Albert Étienne Jean Baptiste Terrien de Lacouperie

The Oldest Book of the Chinese, the Yh-king, and it's Authors

Albert Étienne Jean Baptiste Terrien de Lacouperie

The Oldest Book of the Chinese, the Yh-king, and it's Authors

ISBN/EAN: 9783337168377

Printed in Europe, USA, Canada, Australia, Japan

Cover: Foto ©ninafisch / pixelio.de

More available books at **www.hansebooks.com**

THE OLDEST BOOK OF THE CHINESE

THE YH-KING

AND ITS AUTHORS.

BY

A. TERRIEN DE LACOUPERIE.

Doct. phil. and litt. (Lovan); Laureate of the Acad. Inscr. and B.-L.; Professor of Indo-Chinese Philology (late of Univ. Coll., Lond.) etc.; author of *Origin of the Early Chinese Civilization from Western Sources; The Old Babylonian characters and their Chinese derivates; The Languages of China before the Chinese; Le Non-Monosyllabisme du Chinois antique; Catalogue of Chinese Coins in the British Museum*, etc.; Director of *The Babylonian and Oriental Record;* etc.

VOL. I.

HISTORY AND METHOD

LONDON:
D. NUTT, 270, STRAND.
1892.

THE OLDEST BOOK OF THE CHINESE
AND ITS AUTHORS.

THE OLDEST BOOK OF THE CHINESE

THE YH-KING

AND ITS AUTHORS.

BY

A. TERRIEN DE LACOUPERIE.

Doct. phil. and litt. (Lovan); Laureate of the Acad. Inscr. and B.-L.; Professor of Indo-Chinese Philology (late of Univ. Coll., Lond.) etc.; author of *Origin of the Early Chinese Civilization from Western Sources; The Old Babylonian characters and their Chinese derivates; The Languages of China before the Chinese; Le Non-Monosyllabisme du Chinois antique; Catalogue of Chinese Coins in the British Museum*, etc.; Director of *The Babylonian and Oriental Record;* etc.

VOL. I.

HISTORY AND METHOD

LONDON:
D. NUTT, 270, STRAND.
1892.

HERTFORD:
PRINTED BY STEPHEN AUSTIN AND SONS.

INTRODUCTION.

SUMMARY.—I. How the discovery that the *Yh-King* was based upon old documents and vocabularies has been misunderstood for a foreign origin. II. New translators and writers on the subject since 1883-4. III. Symbolism of *Yh* in *Yh-King*. IV. The *Yh* of *Chöu* was probably an adaptation of parts of the *Kwei-tsang*. V. Instances of very ancient lore hidden in the *Yh-King*.

I.

THE *Yh-King*, the first in rank of the canonical books of China, was the result of a transformation in the twelfth century B.C. of an older work made of documents very ancient in date, and which entitles it to be called the oldest book of the Chinese. I came to that conclusion twelve years ago, and since that time the proofs on which it was based have grown stronger every year. The discrimination of its various strata and sources does away with the apparently insoluble meaning of the work, insolubility shown by the 2,200 or more explanations which have been suggested in China, and the remarkable discrepancies appearing in the European renderings of the text.

The views put forward in several previous papers and in the first part of the present work are simply that the basis of this most abstruse book of the Chinese consisted, for the greater part, of vocabulary lists or *glossarial explanations of* the ideograms forming *the heading of every chapter*, and that these lists had been *framed by the early Chinese leaders* for the benefit and teaching of their followers, in imitation of similar lists used in Anterior Asia, with which they were acquainted, explaining the various uses and meanings of the ideographical characters of the writing which had been taught to them. Now there is a great diffcrence between that contention and an assumed western origin of the work. It has been erroneously and repeatedly stated, at first by *The Athenæum*, Jan. 21, 1882, that we wanted to acknowledge in the *Yh-King*, an Akkadian book, a Babylonian work, or a foreign vocabulary, all statements equally false and inaccurate, as if to throw discredit on our researches.

Although, as shown by the previous exposé, the question of West Asiatic origin of the Chinese civilisation is distinct from the suggested explanation of the *Yh-King*, this side-question (the most important at large, but secondary with special reference to the *Yh-King*) has overshadowed the principal, and the chief point of my views concerning that most ancient Chinese book, viz., that the main portion of it rests on lists of the meanings special to the written symbols headings of the chapters, has been overlooked. In the thoroughly unscientific condition of present sinology, where routine and vested interests take the lead over science, our first communications on the subject could be but variously received. Abused by some, even before anything was published yet, or after the first part of my paper; received scientifically by others, they have been however praised and accepted by not a few independent scholars and colleagues in sinology. In order to avoid personal allusions and remain in the serene atmosphere of scientific research, I refrain mentioning any name. Buried in the fascicula of periodicals my purpose has often been misconceived.

Notwithstanding this unsatisfactory state of things, the little that has been known of the present researches, contemporary with the most disappointing translation by the venerable Dr. J. Legge, in the *Sacred Books of the East*, has awakened a greater and wider interest than could be expected in the matter. Several publications have been made, which we shall notice directly in this introduction. But the awakened interest has not yet received satisfaction, and we may say cannot be satisfied until our new method of translating the *Yh-King* has been proved. In these conditions it has been thought necessary to re-publish separately, as the first part of the present work, the extensive paper of mine which appeared in the *Journal of the Royal Asiatic Society of Great Britain and Ireland*, for 1882-83. The paragraphs 1 to 41 are exactly the same, while the others, viz. 42 to 117 have been slightly altered and improved for a second edition. The actual printing of pp. 1 to 101 was made in 1883, and had remained in sheets at the printers since that time. The pp. 102-121 are new.

II.

The first writer in the field,[1] after the publication of our first articles on the subject, was Dr. J. Edkins, of Peking, in an elaborate article on the *Yh-King as a book of divination*,[2] where he has re-translated from his own point of view with a good deal of extraneous matter the chapters vii. xiii. xv. xx. xxx. and xxxi., translated below (pp. 69-91). His contention is that the work has been devised as a book of divination, and that the internal arrangement of the text and augural words, show a wilful connection with the symbolic meanings attributed to the separate lines composing the *Kwas*. This we are quite disposed to admit, as the result of the transformation undergone by the work under the pencil and interpretation of Wen Wang and Chöu Kung.

The first part of the French translation by Mr. C. L. F. Philastre, mentioned below (p. 49) has appeared in 1885, including the *Kwas* 1 to 30, but the second part with the conclusions of the author have not yet appeared (May 1892). All that has been published is free of anything like the self-

[1] We leave aside the many articles which were only reviews of the subject.
[2] J.R.A.S. 1884, vol. xvi. p. 371, 372.
[3] *Annales du Musée Guimet*, tom viii.

enlightened theories we have mentioned, and deserves all praise. The author has added nothing of himself, being satisfied with a close rendering of the text of the work which he reproduces with the characters, and a copious translation of the wings, besides the extensive commentaries of Cheng tze and of Chou tze, the two famous philosophers of the Sung dynasty.

The fictitious character of the *Yh-King* as a book, and the impossibility of making out any sense by itself, are plainly shown by the rendering of the text, which the author admits in many cases to be words *sans suite*, which can be made out but by the commentaries.

Another French version, complete, has been published by Prof. Ch. de Harlez[1] in 1889. He has given us a perfect *Yh-King*, an ideal work, perhaps more like it might have been than like it ever was. Starting from my discovery that the written character attached to the *Kwa*, and not the *Kwa* itself, is the subject-matter of the chapter, the great orientalist of Louvain has understood the book as a "repertoire de réflexions philosophiques et grammaticales sous 64 titres," and with the help of the commentaries, *Twan* of Wen Wang, and *Siang* of Chöu Kung[2], he has endeavoured to justify his view. Later commentators have also proved useful to his work under that respect. In his very creditable performance he has shown, leaving aside the augural words, that the descriptions, thoughts, and statements of the work in the hands of Wen Wang and Chöu Kung, correspond generally to the meanings and acceptations of the written symbol heading of each chapter. This view differs from ours in that it takes the *Yh* at a later period of its existence than we do, and after it had undergone the transformations, modifications and changes

---

[1] *Cf.* C. de Harlez, *Le texte originaire du Yih King, sa nature sen interprétation*, pp. 35. Journal Asiatique, 1887.—*Le Yih King, texte primitif, retabli, traduit et commenté*, 4to. pp. 155. Bruxelles, 1889.—*Le Yi-King, sa nature et son interpretation*, pp. 164-170 of Journal Asiatique, Jan.-Feb. 1891.

[2] *Cf.* below, pp. 5-6.

of individual characters, the numerous changes in the headings of the chapters, the mutilations of text, and additions of new matters, studied by us, which are traditionally ascribed to Wen Wang. His rendering shows what the latter and Chöu Kung fancied the work was, or ought to be, outside the words and sentences of fortune-telling of which they had largely increased the number; but from the very fact that this aspect of the work corresponds to their own interpretations, it does not follow that tradition is wrong in ascribing its transformation, incomplete and partial as it ever was, to Wen Wang. To describe this temporary stage of the work, while it was in the hands of Wen Wang, as the original or primitive text of the *Yh-King* is therefore a misnomer, since the quotations given in the *Tso chuen* of the *Yh*, previously to this transformation, do not show it in that condition, nor otherwise than already a book of good fortune.

In the *Tsun-nan yat po*, a Chinese journal published at Shang-hai, of which the chief editor is Wang T'ao, the well known Sien Seng, who assisted Dr. J. Legge in his labours on the classics, there is an interesting note concerning the *Yh-King*; and as this note has been translated by the Rev. John Chalmers, I quote from his translation:

". . . . Now according to my judgment, while not expressing any rash opinion as to its Babylonian origin, there must have been some amount of text appended to the names of the hexagrams before the time of King Wan (1100 B.C.). Otherwise, how could Kao-tsung (1200 B.C.) have managed his divinations about 'attacking the Demon regions' (Hexagrams 63, 64), or King Ti-yh, his about "the marriage of his younger sister" (Hexagrams 11, 54) or the Count of Ki, his about 'Injured intelligence' (Hexagrams 36)? Moreover, King Wan and the Duke of Chou were both wise men, and in those paragraphs on the hexagrams and lines ascribed to them, there are absurd and irrelevant phrases combined in a manner which makes it evident that being wise they could only have let them remain out of respect for those who had gone before. And further in the time of King Wan and the Duke of Chou, the *Lien shan* and the *Kwei-tsang* were still extant, and they surely would have made some quotations from them. I send this for information to your paper, in the hope that some Chinese learned in the *Yh* may be induced to throw light on the subject. I may also quote a few words from Mao Si-ho's commentary. He says, 'According to Hwan T'ans *Sui lun*, the *Lien shan* consisted of 80,000 characters, and the Kwei-tsang of 4,300 characters. The former was deposited in Lan t'ai, and the latter in T'ai puh.' Therefore the Hia and Shang dynasties had texts of the Yh (as well as figures). Chăng Kia-tsi (of the Sung dynasty) also says, the *Lien shan* was lost; but there was a commentary on the *Kwei-tsang* by Sze-ma Ying (? Ying-chi) in 13 sections. And finally in the *Tso chwan* and *Kwoh yü* we read frequently of divination in the Shang dynasty. How could they have managed their divination without a text for directions?"

Dr. J. Chalmers adds to the preceding remarks that in his conviction

"The *Yh-King* never was, and never can by any ingenuity be proved to be, more than a hand-book of divination, with the compiling of which King Wan and the Duke of Chou, if they were wise men, had little or nothing to do. The writer of the above paragraph, whoever he is, seems to be working towards the same view. The absurdity and irrelevancy of the greater part of the text cannot be accounted for on any other hypothesis. It can only be compared to Moore's or Zadkiel's almanac. But it is Chinese and not Babylonian."—*China Review*, July, August, 1883, vol. xii. p. 59-60.

With due protest against the mention made by these several writers of a Babylonian origin for the *Yh-King*, which we do not think has ever been put forward, except as an unfair weapon hurled against us, because of our views about the origin from Anterior Asia of the ancient civilisation of China, there is nothing to object on these several views about the oldest book of the Chinese. They disagree with the views of Dr. J. Legge (*cf.* p. 3 note), while they agree with us in several respects. And they leave the question as we have placed it, with the solution which we have proposed, and which the complete translation of the book in the second part of the present work will alone justify and finally establish.

III.

It is certainly singular that the very name of the Book of Changes had became obscure at an early date. The *Shwoh wen* of A.D. 89, which is certainly the oldest etymological dictionary, describes hieroglyphically the symbol *Yh* 易 as representing the Chameleon (*Yen ting*) and house lizard; its appearance being figured by its spelling 'sun and moon' because it symbolizes the ever-changing *Yn* and *Yang*.[1] The philosophical speculations of the Han period had then, as in so many other cases when they combine information,

[1] *Shwoh wen*, s.v. *K'ang hi tze tien*, s.v. Mr. Philastre, l.c. p. 11, wants it to be composed of 日 *sun* and 勿 *not*, which is the modern graphical spelling, but is not the historical etymology.

traditional and speculative, the better of the sober etymologist. In the critical edition of the *Shwoh wen* issued in 1833, the definition of *lizard* only is preserved[1], and this agrees certainly with the hieroglyphic appearance, more wilfully suggestive than traditional, of several of the ancient forms of the symbol.[2] The unsophisticated fact is simply that the tradition about the genuine composition of the original character was partly lost, and that in the ideographism which prevailed since the renovation of writing of 820, Chinese scribes were wont to discern at any cost a hieroglyphism, traditional or invented, in every written character. The antecedent character in the mother writing of Anterior Asia has happily been identified and permits us to say that it was composed of *Star*,[3] with another character meaning sky, stone, etc.[4]

IV.

The *Chöu Li* or Ritual of the Chöu dynasty states that the *Ta p'u* or Great Augur has charge of the rules of the three *Yh* 易, called respectively *Lien shan, Kwei tsang,* and *Chöu Yh*; each having eight *Kwas* and eight combinations of them. Therefore the term *Yh* was chiefly attached to the sixty-four *Kwas* and the texts attached to them. But the texts of the *Lien shan* and *Kwei-tsang* were different under some respects from those of the *Chöu Yh*, if we may judge from the quotations of the last named work which are met with in encyclopedic literature. The difference consisted not in the written symbol attached to each *Kwa* and object-matter of every chapter, nor in the series of its meanings and acceptations, but in the additional statements which followed them, and were historical or legendary allusions.

---

[1] A lizard. The other meanings of this character are given by phonetic usage. J. Chalmers, *The structure of Chinese Characters, after the Shwoh wan*, 100 A.D., *and the Phonetic Shwoh wan*, 1833.—1882, *p.* 157.

[2] *Cf.* Min Tsi-k'ih, *Luh shu tung*, Kiv. 10, f. 14, and for *tin*, f. 7.

[3] *i.e.* ANA NANU. — *Cf.* A. Amiaud L. Mechineau, *Tableau Comparé des écritures Babylonienne et Assyrienne Anciennes et Modernes*, 1887, No. 17.— R. Brunnow, *Cuneiform classified list*, Nos. 448-453.—T. de L., in B. O. R., vol. v. p. 39.

[4] *Chöu li, Tchun Kwan, Ta p'u;* Kiv. 24, f. 4, 5; tr. Biot, vol. ii. p. 70, 71.

The quotations made in the *Tso chuen* at the occasion of divinations by twigs of the milfoil are most instructive about the history of the *Yh-King*. In eleven cases the Yh of Chöu is referred to *eo nomine*, and fragments of the text or explanations clearly derived from it are quoted. In eight cases no name of work is given, the author mentioning only which *Kwas* were drawn from the milfoil before proceeding to quote texts following them. Now the interest lies in these texts. In 530 and 548 B.C., they are exactly as if quoted from the Yh of Chöu, and taking their respective late dates into consideration, we may assume that the non-mention there of its name is only an oversight of the writer. On the other hand, in 645 (1) and 575 B.C. the texts quoted are not found in the Yh of Chöu at all, while in 662, 660, 645 (2) and 635 B.C. parts only of the texts quoted in each instance have survived in it. The outstanding fractions belong in most cases to historical allusions, like those referred to in the *Kwei-tsang*, but different as to the facts spoken of. Now as seven quotations only of the latter work are available for comparison with five of the unknown work whose extracts appear in the *Tso-Chuen*, the fact that none of them correspond is no proof that they do not belong to one and the same work in one hundred and twenty-eight sections. There is on the contrary every reason to suppose that the unnamed work was the *Kwei-tsang*, which, belonging to the preceding and little respected dynasty, remained nameless out of reverence for the ruling family of Chöu who had also a book of changes, not available yet in these States.

The *Kwei-tsang* is said to have contained 4300 words, subdivided into sixty-four chapters, each having a upper and lower part corresponding therefore to the double section of every *Kwa*.[2] This is the length of the *Yh* of Chöu, and there

---

[1] *Cf.* below part i. § 18.
[2] The exact number of characters in the *Yh-King*, without the commentaries or wings, is 4134 divided into 448 sentences from 2 to 30 characters, in 64 chapters, from 30 to 95 each. With the wings the total number is 24,107.

is now little doubt in our mind that the latter work is nothing else than a modification and adaptation of parts of the first by Wen Wang. While secluded at Yü-li, he has suppressed the historical allusions which referred to a period too remote in time, and has substituted to them references to events of later date with which his people was acquainted, and a larger number of augural sentences and foretelling words in conformity with some views of his own about the respective symbolism of the two component parts of every *Kwa*. On the other alterations and allusions introduced by himself and the Duke of Chöu into the work, enough has been said in paragraphs 38–41 of the present volume.

There is no doubt possible that a former *Yh* was in the hands of Wen Wang, and that he played havoc right and left with the text, which however he preserved as groundwork of his own *Yh*. Historical allusions have been lost beyond recovery by suppression of a part of the state ment, or have been suppressed altogether as proved by the quotations of the *Tso Chuen* in 645(1) and 575 B.C. An instance of partial suppression of such a text will explain what I mean. In 645(2) a divination by the Milfoil is made, and the Kwas drawn were the 54th and the 38th; extracts are given from the texts following them. The Augurer says amongst other statements: "there is defeat in Tsêng Kiu," 敗于宗丘 Now in Wen Wang's arrangement of the text it has been simplified to two words: 厥宗 in which it is not surprising that every one of the European exegetes hitherto engaged in interpreting the work has failed to recognize there what it is, *i.e.* an allusion to the defeat inflicted by Hwang-ti upon Tcheh-yeu at Tseng Kiu, which defeat is mentioned in full in the original text of the *Yh* of the Shang dynasty (otherwise the *Kwei-tsang*).

In some cases the arranger of the *Yh* of Chöu does not

---

[1] *Tso chuen*, Hi Kung, xv, 13.
[2] *Cf.* Pih Yuan's gloss. on the *Shan hai King*, Kiv. 17, f. 3 v.

seem to have always understood the original purpose of the texts he was using, as shown by the fact that his separation into chapters does not coincide in every case with the change of subject matter; for instance, line 6 of chapter lxi belongs to chapter lxii, lines 1 and 2 of chapter xlii belong to chapter xli, etc.

In re-arranging the *Yh* (of the Shang Dynasty) for the use of their followers, the Chöu leader suppressed the allusions which it contained to events of oldest times, and inserted in their stead references to events and circumstances of recent dates and well-known in his time. Such for instance as the allusions to Kao tsung (1364-1324 B.C.) and his campaign against the Kwei fang (*Kwa*, 63, l. 2, and 64, l. 4); to Ti-y, the last ruler but one of the Shang-Yn Dynasty (*Kwa* 12, l. 5 and 54, l. 5); to Ki-tze (*Kwa*, 36, l. 5); to Mount K'i the traditional residence of the Chöu (*Kwa* 46, l. 4 and 17, l. 6). Except in one case (*Kwa* 63, l. 3) all these allusions are placed in the second part of each chapter, *i.e.*, line 4, 5, and 6, and thus justify the view we have expressed with reference to the relative position of the vocabulary and examples in the ancient documents.

V.

It is not sufficient to be acquainted with the languages and philosophy of the Chinese to understand the *Yh-King*; much more is required.[1] The descriptions of the ideograms, their meanings and instances of their use, which form the original text, are full of ancient lore, which in our ignorance we are open to misconceive and mistranslate. In the complete translation which forms the second part of the present work, not a few passages are still obscure, and we may consider

[1] I apply here to the *Yh-King* and slightly modified, the judgment passed on Mr. H. A. Giles' *The Remains of Lao-tze retranslated*, by Prof. Georg van der Gabelentz of Berlin, when he said that a knowledge of the language and a philosophical training do not suffice to gain a correct understanding of the *Tao teh King*. (*China Review*, vol. xvii.)

that the necessary elucidations historical, mythological and otherwise are wanting.¹

I beg to submit here a few cases in support of my statements concerning the existence in the *Yh-King* of many references to ancient lore and customs.

The first chapter which concerns *Kien* 乾 *Heaven*, and is one of the most conspicuous by the unintelligibleness of all the renderings, contains some cosmogonic allusions, non-confucianist in character, and therefore ignored by the literati. They refer to the five dragons, 五龍, *Wu Lung* of the fabulous speculations concerning the mythological ages. The second of the ten *Ki* was that of these five dragons in the general scheme of olden times.²

In the said chapter we find them mentioned as follows:

l. 1: 潛龍勿用; *i.e.*, the *Ts'ien Lung*, were in no distinct place.

l. 2: 見丨在田; *i.e.* the *Kien Lung* were in the lands.

l. 4: 或躍(丨)³在淵; the *Hwoh-yoh* (*Lung*) were in the watery deep.

l. 5: 飛丨在天; the *Fei Lung* were in the skies.

l. 6: 亢丨有悔; (and) the *K'ang Lung* (when) a change occurred.⁴

The second chapter contains two important fragments of their most ancient lore, both in the first line. The object of the symbol 坤 *Kw'en* described is *the earth*,—literally from the ideographism of the character, the stretched earth—or passive element of nature.

Now *Kw'en*, 坤⁵ in the first line, is described as 牝馬之貞⁶

¹ Dr. J. Edkins has made a remark to that effect in his mentioned paper, *i.e.*, p. 380, when he says: "If in certain passages it (the *Yh-King*) is obscure, it ought to be considered whether the necessary historical elucidations are wanting."
² *Cf.* W. F. Mayers, *Chinese Readers Manual*, p. 364.
³ The word *Lung* has been dropped here because of the rhythm.
⁴ The *Kwang-ya* says that there were five sorts of dragons. So said Kwantze in the seventh century B.C.
⁵ In the former *Yh* or *Kwei tsang*, this character was written 巺, *cf. Khang hi tze tien*, Tze wei p'u, cl. 12.
⁶ Translated: "correct and having the firmness of a mare" (Legge).—bien et perfection de la jument (Philastre).

i.e. "the firmness of the female horse," a statement utterly unintelligible, did we not remember that in the earliest cosmogony with which the civilisers of China were acquainted, the primitive being, the root of Heaven and Earth, was a female animal.¹

The second fragment, referred to in the same chapter, runs as follows: 西南得朋東北喪朋, *i.e.* "the South-West got the falling down, the North-East lamented for it,"² where we cannot help recognising a clear allusion to the mythological circumstance of the deluge legend as adapted³ and preserved in China, where the story says that the four pillars of the earth sundered, and the earth became defective on one side. A chief difference in the present rendering is that 朋 is an early and undeveloped form of 崩 to fall down as a mountain, and not the symbol for a pair or friends.

The Troglodytes people, spoken of in the thirteenth chapter,⁴ translated as a specimen in the first part of the present work (p. 89, 91) are no other than the cave men who inhabited the Loess of the present Shen-si and Shansi provinces, when the Bak families arrived there from the west, a practice which, required by the soil, is followed to the present day.⁵

¹ It was the earliest cosmogony of Babylonia, anterior to the speculations on the male and female principles, which the Bak sings had learned before their arrival in N.W. China. It was preserved in a work containing many traditions alleged to have been handed down from the time of Hu Nak-Kunte (Yu Nai Hwang-ti) the leader of the Bak sings, and preserved in the Royal Archives. Lao-tze when Keeper of those Archives became acquainted with it and introduced it in his *Tao teh King*, Kiv. 6. Lieh-tze Kiv. 1, 1 C has also quoted it. For the Babylonian texts, *cf.* A. H. Sayce, *Religion of the Ancient Babylonians*, pp. 262, 375.—On the whole question cf. my work on the *Origin of the early Chinese Civilisation*, ch. viii. 141-146.

² Translated previously, whatever it may mean—"getting friends in the south-west, and losing friends in the north-east (Legge)"—"Il pourracquerir des amis d'un côté, mais il les perdra de l'autre" (De Harlez).—"Dans le sud-ouest possibilité d'avoir des amis ; dans le Nord-est perte des amis." (Philastre).

³ *Cf.* my monograph, *The Deluge tradition and its remains in Ancient China*, part I. 26, and §§ 135-139 below the change of Orientation.

⁴ Under the heading 同 *Tung-jen* the symbol *t'ung* was originally the picture of a *crucible* (whence "mixed together,") as shown by its regular derivation from the mother writing of Western Asia. Cf. the *Ku-wen* forms in *Min Tsi-Kih*, *Luh shu t'ung*, and Amiaud-Mechineau, *Tableau comparé des Ecritures Babylonienne Assyrienne Archaiques et Modernes*, 1887. No. 68.

⁵ Cf. for instance F. von Richtofen, China, vol. i. 1877, pp. 68, 72, 73, 96, 199, 117.

In matters of exchange and currency, the Bak families used to barter all commodities, besides wrought and unwrought metal by weight; arriving in the Flowery Land they found among the native populations of the east a currency of shells and cowries which they adapted to their own use and requirements in dealing with them.[1] Now this early currency is referred to twice in the *Yh-King*.

Under the XLIst *Kwa* originally 員 *yuen* round things,[2] now a classifier of cowries (money and goods), l. 6-5, we find: 或 益 之 十 朋 之 龜, "also added to ten pairs of tortoise shells."[3]

Under the LIst *Kwa*, originally *Li* 籃, regulate, central, number, bestow, give orders,[4] at the line 2 mention is made of 億 喪 貝, *i.e.*, 100,000 dead shells or cowries.[5] The statement is particularly interesting as it shows that when it was at first put into writing for the instruction of the people, the author thought necessary to explain the matter to his followers still unfamiliar with the practice. It has altogether escaped the attention of translators.

A great danger in explaining the *Yh-King* is to take as *bona-fide* expressions and meanings in the language, such acceptations of words which have no earlier existence than this work itself, and no other meaning than that which have been attributed to them by the ancient commentaries whence

---

[1] *Catalogue of Chinese coins including those in the British Museum*, introd. p. vii. viii. and page 582 *On the Metallic cowries of Ancient China*, p. 438. (J.R.A.S. 1888, vol. xx.) *Primitive Currency of Ancient China*, § 7.

[2] In the modern text, 損 *sun*, diminish, injure, destroy, has been substituted to it, to match the symbolical meaning of the hexagram, which, however, could not be got at in all cases; whence the incongruity of the chapter. Cf. below, § 39.

[3] Cf. Legge's translation . . . shows parties adding to (the stores of) its subject ten pairs of tortoise shells . . . and Dr. Harlez: "Augmenter les biens quelqu'un par le riches presents (litt. de tortues à vingt écailles?"
When the work was recast, the character 龜 was substituted to it. Cf. below § 39. On the latter character of Min-Tsih-ki, *Luh shu t'ung*, Kiv. 7, fol. 53; on *Li* ibid i. 28.

[5] There are two varieties of cowries, the "live cowries," and the "dead cowries." Cf. Ed. Balfour, *Encyclopædia of India*, 1885, vol. i. p. 835. This particularity explains the statement on the line 5 of the same *Kwa* where reference is made to " 100,000 not dead."

they have taken an undue hold in the literature. Therefore little value can be attached to their case, and the instances are most numerous.

A danger of another sort is to translate by their modern acceptations expressions which at the time when the work was composed had a different meaning. For instance, in chap. iii. 1. 6-21, under the heading 屯 *tun*, occurs the statement 乘 馬 班 如 *sheng ma pan ju*,[1] which a quotation of the *Tso tchuen* in 661 B.C. explains as meaning "carriages and horses follow one another."[2] At present *sheng ma* means to ride a horse,[3] and these two words have been translated accordingly in some European translations,[4] as if their authors were unaware of the pre-cited rendering, and as if they did not know that riding on horseback was not yet the custom at that time. The oldest instance of this improvement in China occurred only in 517 B.C.[5]; therefore such a translation is not exact.

[1] The word *pan* there is also written 般. Cf. T.P.Y.L. Kiv. 893, f. 2.
[2] *Tso tchuen*, Min Kung, i. 5. *Chin. Class.* vol. v. p. 125.
[3] *Sheng ma*, in equum ascendere (Basil.); to mount a horse (Stent, *Pek. voc.*) The symbol *sheng* as shown by some of its ancient forms was intended to suggest a chariot with two horses. Cf. Min Tsi-kih, *Luh shu tung*, iv. 33 v.
[4] The four characters pre-cited are translated: Montant à cheval et comme demeurant en rang (Philastre); un cheval Monté qui recule (De Harlez); *even* the horses of her chariot *also* seem to be retreating (J. Legge).
[5] Cf. *Tso tchuen*, Tch'ao Kung, xxv. 7. *Khang hi tze tien* s.v. 驥 In former times, men did not ride on horse back; it came into practice towards the end of the Chöu dynasty (Gloss. to the *Li Ki*). Liu hiuen commenting upon the statement pre-cited of the *Tso chuen*, said that it was the first instance of riding on horseback (*K'i*). The first use of cavalry in warfare in China dates of the time of Su Ts'in, *i.e.* 350 B.C. (*Tcheng tze tung*), *ibid*. At the battle of Marathon (490 B.C.) the Persians but not the Greeks as yet were using cavalry. Riding on horseback was only occasional at the Homeric (*Odyss.* v. 371; *Iliad*, x. 513, xv. 679), and Vedic (*Rig.* v. 61-2) periods. Cf. O. Schrader *Prehistoric Antiquities*, p. 262; Max Müller, *Biographies of Words*, p. 116. From the time of Solomon, says Dr. C. F. Keil, *Manual of Biblical Archæology*, ii. 219, kings and nobles used horses for riding and driving instead of asses and mules (2 Kings, ix. 21, 23; xi. 16; Isa. xxx. 16; Amos, iv. 10), but this assertion seems doubtful so far as riding on horseback is concerned before the time of Isaiah, as the three first passages do not refer to it. Horses existed in Egypt as early as the time of Jacob (Gen. xlvii. 17; Exod. ix. 3; Deut. xvii. 16), and appear on the monuments from the time of Thothmes I. On the question *Why was the horse driven before it was ridden?* cf. Dr. Isaac Taylor, *The Origin of the Aryans*, 1890, p. 161, and the letters of M. M. William Ridgeway, M. L. Herbert McClure, F. Max Müller, Talfourd Ely, in *The Academy* of Jan. 3, 10, 17, 24, and Feb. 14, 1891.

Such is the mode of investigation pursued here in view of arriving at a clearer intelligence of the *Yh-King*, and that which will be exemplified in the translation, which, with the valuable help of Prof. R. K. Douglas, will form the second volume of the present work.

I may be permitted to present here my best thanks for the valuable help I have received from several scholars and friends: Dr. R. Rost, Librarian of the India Office, for the loan of books under his care; Mr. T. G. Pinches, of the Department of Oriental Antiquities (British Museum), for MS. notes; Prof. R. K. Douglas, for his constant support; and the late Mr. E. C. Baber, Chinese Secretary of H.B.M. Legation at Peking, for his valuable assistance and advice in the correction of the proofs. The whole paper was written in August, 1882, but the second part (§§ 42-117) was revised in March, 1883. I subjoin a few *corrigenda* and *addenda* to the first part:—Introduction, last note: The criticism of Dr. Legge's *Yh-King* by Prof. R. K. Douglas appeared in *The Academy* of Aug. 12th (not July 12th). Dr. Legge wrote a letter about it (Sept. 30), and Prof. Douglas replied, maintaining his views (Oct. 7). *The Athenæum* (Sept. 2, No. 2862) published a review by a well-known sinologist of Dr. Legge's *Yh-King*, in which he said: "We cannot catch the inspiration that gave to Dr. Legge the 'clue to the interpretation' of this obscure book;" and further, "We have . . . . to confess that we do not understand its drift or its interpretation." The same scientific and literary journal published in its following issue (Sept. 9th, No. 2863) a letter of mine in answer to the unjustified and sharp attack made against me by Dr. Legge in his Preface, pp. xviii and xix to the XVIth vol. of the *Sacred Books of the East*. Dr. Legge replied in the issue of Sept. 23, No. 2865, and the controversy was brought to a close by another letter of mine maintaining my views, published Sept. 30th, No. 2866. I subjoin a list of Addenda and Corrigenda.

§ 11 (*f*) : A learned correspondent has suggested that 交易 and 得其所 are two well-known colloquial expressions; but certainly they are not in this case, being reproduced from old. Cf. also *Yuen Kien luy han*, R, 192, f. 24, v. The phrase means that Shen-nung casts lots in order to attribute to the changes (易) their respective place.

§ 13 : 'subreptitiously,' misprinted ' surreptitiously.'

§ 14 (*l*) : The same above-quoted correspondent has suggested rightly that 益 ought not to be taken here as a verb, but as an adverb. We should substitute the following translation : "He (Wen Wang) being imprisoned at Yu-li, then, increased the changes proper to the eight Kwas, in favour of the 64 Kwas." This would agree with the statements of Hwrng P'u Mih and of Lo-Pi, in his work about the 九 and 六 lines.

p. 16, § 19. The oldest instance on record, that I know, of a divination by the *Yh* of Chöu, is that of 705 B.C., when *Li* the thirteenth Kung of *Ch'en* (in Honan) sent especially to Chöu for that purpose. The Kwas drawn were *Kwan* (20) and *P'i* (12) (Szema Tsien, *She ki*, Kiv. 36, f. 2 v.). The next instances mentioned in history are those of 672 and 602 which we have noticed below (p. 16) when the work was still in the hands of officers of Chöu, and it was only in 597 that separate copies of the *Chöu Yh* were in circulation.

p. 78, § 95. Herewith the translations of Mr. P. L. F. Philastre (1885) and of Prof. C. de Harlez (1889), which have appeared since our text was printed, and which I submit for comparison with those of P. Regis, Rev. MacClatchie and Dr. Legge, pp. 78–80; version of Mr. P. L. F. Philastre : *Li*, avantage de la perfection ; liberté ; réunir des vaches, *présage henreux*.

l. 1-9.—Démarche héritante ; absence de culpabilité.

l. 6-2.—Clarté jaune ; *grandeur du présage henreux*.

l. 9-3.—Clarté du soleil qui décline ; ne pas frapper sur la terre cuite et chanter ; formuler des lamentations sur la grande vieillesse ; présage malheureux.

l. 9-4.—Comme un courant rapide, de même il vient ; comme brûlant, comme mort, comme abandonné.

l. 6-5.—Comme versant des larmes qui coulent ; comme triste et se lamentant ; *présage henreux*.

l. Upper 9.—Le roi se dispose à partir en guerre ; il a des succès, il choisit des chefs ; ce qu'il capture n'est pas le vulgaire ; pas de culpabilité.

Prof. C. de Harlez : *Li*, beauté "bel exterieur," se développe et s'achève comme dans l'élève d'un animal domestique (qui, bien, saigné, est gras, bean, luisant).

1.—Lorsque la conduite est fautive, mais qu'on cherche avec soin à la rectifier, en évitera tout blâme.

2.—Le plus bel éclat est celui du jaune.

3.—Lorsque l'éclat du soleil est à son déclin, ce n'est plus la joix qu'il inspire, mais la tristesse. (Litt, ou ne fait plus de musique au moyen des instruments de terre, ni en chantant, mais c'est le gémissement d'un vieillard. Le tout indique la déchéance et le chagrin qu'elle cause). Com.

ADDENDA AND CORRIGENDA. xxi

4.—La lumière du feu apparaît subitement ; elle brûle, donne la mort ; on ne peut la supporter (App.)

5.—Quand le prince se met en expedition, on verse des larmes et pousse des gémissements. Et cela doit étre car il sort pour aller châtier les rebelles et les méchants ; dans ses *brillants* exploits il brise les têtes des chefs et reçoità merci ceux qui ne se sout point associés à leur révolte, Ainsi il n'encourt ancun blâme.—Cf. P. L. F. Philastre, *Le Yi-King*, I., p. 478-488. C. de Harlez, *Le Yih-King*, p. 78-79.

Both translators have largely made use of the commentaries to make something of the text. At the line 9-4, Mr. Philastre says in a note after "courant rapide"—"le sens n'est explicable que par la tradition et par la valeur qu'elle attribuee à ces mots, en apparence sans suite." *Ibid.* p. 485. Prof. C. de Harlez refers to the appendices or commentaries for every one of the lines.

Dr. J. Edkins, in his paper on *The Yi-King as a book of divination*, has re-translated from his point of view which we have explained iu the introduction, the six chapters given by us as specimens, but with a good deal of extraneous matter. I extract all the passages which may be looked upon as his translation of this thirtieth Kwa *Li*, for the sake of comparison with the translations of P. Regis, Rev. MacClatchie, Dr. J. Legge, and of Mr. Philastre and Prof. C. de Harlez.

Herewith Dr. J. Edkins' rendering : *Li*. Correct conduct insures continued success. In nourishing the cow (a patient and docile animal, here introduced as a symbol of submission) luck will be insured.

1.—The shoe or your stepping is entangled or confused. Be careful. There will be no error.

2.—The yellow Li bird. Great good fortune.

3.—The shining of the setting sun is the symbol. If not saluted by beating earthen pans and singing, there will be heard the sighing of the tottering old man. The omen is unfortunate.

4.—He comes with sudden rush, like the burning of a fire, like death, as if to be rejected.

5.—Weakness on the throne. A shower of tears shows how sad he is. He will have good fortune.

6.—The King in action. He leads out an army. He obtains fame. He kills the chiefs, and merely make prisoners of those who were not follow rebels.—J.R.A.S, 1884, vol. xvi. p. 371-372.

p. 28, note 1. The allusion to the battle of Hwang-ti in *Fan-ts-'üen* (not *ts'iun*) is interesting because it shows how ancient and deeply rooted among the Chinese traditions was the legendary account of Hwang-ti, which otherwise might have been supposed to be a late importation, cf. for this legend : T. de L., *The Chinese Mythical Kings and the Babylonian Canon* 1883. *From Ancient Chaldæa and Elam to early China* 1891, par 46. The Tchi-yeu episode, *ibid.* is also alluded to in a sentence from the *Kwei-tsang*. Cf. *Shan-hai-king*, edit. Pih-Yuan, xvii, 3 v.

p. 29, note 2. Other extracts of the *Kwei-tsang* are given in the *Tai ping yü lan*, Kiv. 35, fol. 1, and in the Shan hai king, edit. Pih-Yuan, 1781 ; one Kiv. 2, f. 14 ; two Kiv. 7, f. 1; one Kiv. 17, f. 3, v. Kiv. 929, f. 1, etc.

p. 74. The Kim (mod. Kien) spoonbill bird was known to the Bak families, before their coming in the east, as shown by the fact that the Chinese name is a loan word from the west. Cf. Egyptian *us* and *Khemi*, *Khem*, Babylonian *Kumû*, Assyrian *atân na'ari*, she ass of the rivers; in W. Houghton, *The Birds of the Assyrian Monuments and Records*, pp. 95, 140; and *The bird originally denoted by the English word Pelican.—The Academy*, April 5, 1884, p. 244.

p. 90. Perhaps ought we read 犬戎 instead of 伏戎, and thus find the Küen Jung Aborigines of which much is said during the Chöu dynasty.

p. 96, § 109. We may add the following instances of similar perversions :—When commentators arose to explain the Unadisutras, they found the greater part of the words contained in them still employed in the literature of their age, or recorded in older dictionaries. But an unknown residuum remained, and to these whenever tradition failed them, they were bold enough to assign arbitrary significations (Aufrecht). In Mexico wilful changes of meaning of phrases were introduced in the recitation of traditional songs by the initiated. Cf. Adolf. Bastian, *Sprachvergleichende studien*, 1870, pp. 27n, 61.

p. 96, § 110. On the name of Bak (= Pak or Pöh in Pöh sing) as an ethnic. Cf. *The Languages of China before the Chinese*, 1887, § 200-201; and additions in French edition, 1888, p. 159. *Origin of the Early Chinese civilisation*, chap. v.

p. 96, § 110. On the derivation of the Chinese characters from the ancient script of Babylonia and Elam. Cf. T. de L. : *The old Babylonian characters and their Chinese derivates* 27, pp. March, 1888 (B. and O. R. vol. ii), and the approbative article of Prof. A. H. Sayce on the same subject in *Nature*, June 7, 1888, and B. and O. R. August, 1888. T. de L., *Chips of Babylonian and Chinese Palæography ibid.* Oct. 1888. *From Ancient Chaldæa and Elam to Early China*, par. 14-32; B. and O. R. vol. v., Feb. 1891; *Catalogue of Chinese Coins*, introduction, pp. 33-34; *Beginnings of writing*, chap. ix. 1892. C. J. Ball, *The New Accadian*, 1889-90 pass.; *Ideograms common to Accadian and Chinese*, 1890-91, 23 and 15 pp.

p. 97, No. 111. For the similarity of method about ideological lists, Cf. for instance the list of 24 terms for Ruler in Babylonia (W. R. T. ii., 33-3) and the first and second lists in the Oct-ya.

ERRATA.

- P. 4, l. 7, *after* which *add* (out of 2240).
- ,, 9, l. 11, *for* 蠧 *read* 蕾.
- ,, ,, l. 31, *for* writings *read* writing.
- ,, ,, n. 1, for *Li tai Wang nien piao* read *Li tai Ti Wang nien piao.*
- ,, 11, l. 26, *for* 沁 *read* 泌
- ,, 12, l. 2, *for* 入 *read* 八
- ,, ,, l. 4, *for* 末 *read* 未
- ,, 13, l. 32, *for* 十卦 *read* 十四卦
- ,, 16, l. 33, *for* or the Siang *read* or from the *Ssiang*.
- ,, 24, n. 2, l. 7, *after* Mencius *add* III., 2, ix. 8.
- ,, 29, n. 2, l. 5, *after* reproduce *add* some of.
- ,, 33, l. 10, *for* a girl *read* an aunt.
- ,, 34, l. 27, *for* 无 *read* 先
- ,, 36, l. 10, *for* fanciful *read* fancied.
- ,, 39, l. 27, *for* Kin *read* Kiu.
- ,, 41, l. 2, *for* Se-Ma *read* Sa-ma.
- ,, ,, l. 10, *for* Lin Hiang *read* Liu Hiang.
- ,, 42, l. 7, 8, *for* chang Hüan *read* Ch'eng Hiuen.
- ,, 44. l. 17, *after* Ch'eng Kang Ch'eng *add* or Ch'eng Hiuen.
- ,, 53, l. 14, *for* in modern writing *read* in modern text.
- ,, 56, l. 8, *for* from *read* form.
- ,, 74, §. 74, *add note*, For the geography of these and other equivalences, cf. T. de L., *The Languages of China before the Chinese.* §§. 53-57.

CONTENTS.

I.—DESCRIPTION OF THE BOOK.—§§ 1. General description of the book. —2. The Kwas as a classification.—3. Commentaries commonly embodied with the text.—4. Authors of the *Twan* and *Siang*.— 5. Characteristics of the ten wings.—6. The first two wings.—7. Length of the book.

II.—ANCIENT TEXTS ON THE AUTHORSHIP OF THE BOOK.—§§ 8. Vulgar attribution.—9. Statements in cheap and modern books.—10. Texts on the authorship of the Kwas.—11. The supposed work of Shen-Nung.—12. Statements by Wang Fu-mi.—13. Statements by Lo-Pi.—14. The *Hi-tze* does not support Wen Wang's authorship.—15. Nor does Se-ma Tsien.—16. Se-ma Tsien on Confucius. —17. Statement in the Tso-Chuen on Chöu-Kung.—18. Quotations of the Yh in the Tso-Chuen.—19. Their chronology.—20. Prove the progress of the Yh.—21. Prove the existence of the Yh text before Wen Wang.—22. No proof whatever of the authorship of Wen Wang.

III.—INFLUENCE OF THE EVOLUTION OF WRITING.—§§ 23. The old Chinese writing, its early phoneticism and its decay.—24. The hieroglyphical revival about 820 B.C.—25. The unification by Ts'in She-Hoang-ti.—26. The transcriptions are made ideographically. —27. The addition of ideographical determinatives or keys.

IV.—OBVIOUS VESTIGES OF THE OLD TEXT.—§§ 28. The Lo map and Lo writing.—29. The Kwas.—30. The prognostics slips in the Shu-King.—31 The *Kwei-tsang* and the *Lien-shan*.—32. The old text in the Tso Chuen.—33. Differences of style in the text of the Yh.—34. The foretelling words outside the rhymes.—35. The Ku-wen text.—36. Ways and means to find it out.—37. Ancient characters of the old text.—38. Characters changed. Examples.— 39. Changes in the headings of the chapters.—40. Changes in the transcriptions.—41. Importance of the changes.

V.—THE NATIVE INTERPRETATIONS.—§§ 42. Stupendous number of interpreters.—43. Modifications introduced by Wen Wang.—44. How he classified the old documents.—45. Impossibility for a man of common sense to write it.—46. The *Yh* handed down by the disciples of Confucius.—47. Editions and commentaries in the Former Han annals.—48. Commentaries known at the Han period. 49. Other commentators.—50. The *Yh* and alchemy.—51. Other commentaries.—52. Commentators of the Sung period.—53. Critics of the present dynasty.—54. The interpreters much more numerous than here quoted.—55. Curious modern views of the Chinese.

VI.—THE EUROPEAN INTERPRETATIONS.—§§. 56. Fragmentary translations of PP. Premare, Couplet, Visdelou.—57. Fragmentary versions of M. J. P. Schumacher, Dr. O. Piper, Adolf Helfferich, etc., etc., P. Zottoli.—58. Complete Latin version of P. Regis and others.—59. Mystic French version by Mr. P. L. F. Philastre.—60. Complete English version by Rev. MacClatchie.—61. Complete English version by Dr. J. Legge.—62. He has made a Yh-King of his own fashion.—63. Curious effect of these made-up interpretations.—64. How they have been obtained.—65. They are complete nonsense, and cannot be genuine.

VII.—COMPARISON OF THE INTERPRETATIONS.—§§ 66. Great number of unwarranted special meanings.—67. Curious example of *T'ien* 'heaven' translated *shaving*.—68. Example of the 8th chapter.—69. Passage quoted in the Tso-chuen.—70. Another passage in the same work.—71. Fancy of the translations.—72. *Id.*

VIII.—METHODS OF INTERPRETATION.—§§ 73. Process followed by Wen Wang.—74. The author of the *Sü Kwa* has nearly guessed the clue.—75. The Yh has never been lost.—76. Method by modification of the characters.—77. The guess-at-the-meaning principle of translation.—78. In what it consists.—79. The duty of a translator.—80. Mencius has not upheld the guess-at-the-meaning principle.—81. Those views are based on a delusion about the archaic Chinese.—82. The scientific method of translation.

IX.—TRANSLATIONS FROM THE *Yh.*—§§. 83. Characteristics of the text.—84. Foretelling formula interpolated.—85. Remarks on several characters.—86. Our view of the *Yh.*—87. Reasons for giving six chapters as specimens.—88. Remarks on the VIIth chapter, *Sze.*—89. Meaning of *Sze* in the Classics.—90. Translation.—91. It is a vocabulary.—92. The XVth chapter, *Kien*, a vocabulary.—93. Translation.—94. The XXXth chapter, *Li*, a vocabulary.—95. Translation.—96. The XXXIst chapter, *Kan*, a vocabulary.—97. Translation.—98. The XXth chapter, *Kwan*, mixed, vocabulary and ballad.—99. Translation.—100. The XIIIth chapter, *Tung jen*, ethnographical.—101. Translation.—102. The foretelling-words outside the rhymes.

X.—CONTENTS FORGOTTEN OF THE *Yh.*—§§ 103. Contents of the *Yh.*—104. How made up of sundry old documents.—105. When it was arranged.—106. Is nothing else than a vocabulary.—107. Other examples of books forgotten.—108. The Japanese Nihongi. 109. The Oupnehkat.

XI.—ORIGIN OF THE YH-KING.—§§ 110. Affinities of the writings and institutions of China and S.W. Asia.—111. Similarity of ideographical and phonetic lists of words.—112. Notion of syllabaries borrowed from the West.—113. Comparison of the characters *lu* and *li.*—114. Distance in time and space of the documents compared.—115. The cuneiform syllabaries and the Chinese *Œt-ya.*—116. Some western texts may have been preserved in China.—117. Important value of the *Yh-king* for ancient Chinese research.

XII.—MATERIAL HISTORY OF THE YH-KING.—§ 118. The text *Ku-wen* engraved on wood tablets, and *chuen* painted with lacquer on bamboo slips.—119. After 212 B.C. written in *Li-shu* with the hair pencil on silk cloth.—120. The old lacquered tablets were finally destroyed in 311 A.D.—121. The *Ku-wen*, *chuen*, and *Li-shu* texts engraved on stone tablets in 175 A.D.—122. The *Li-shu* text engraved again on stone tablets before 265 A.D.—123. Out of 144 tablets only 50 remained in 600 A.D.—124. Texts printed in 593, 717, and all the classics in 932 A.D.—125. Preservation by print of parts of the ancient texts.—126. The present character was substituted for the former *Li-shu* in 744.—127. New stone classics erected in 833 at Chang-ngan, and in the last century at Peking.

I.—*Concluding chapter.*—THE YH-KING AND THE WESTERN ORIGIN OF THE CHINESE CIVILISATION.—§ 128. Relationship of the Chinese with the Turano-Scythian languages.—129. Present scheme of these languages.—130. Cousinship and Antiquity of the Chinese and Akkado-Sumerian.

II.—§ 131. The Bak families were northern neighbours of the Akkado-Sumerians at first uncivilized.—132. The Bak families claimed their independence *c.* 2332 B.C.—133. Arrived in N.W. China *c.* 2882 B.C.; the Bak families wrote documents.—134. Numerous proofs of this western origin.

III.—§ 135. Derivation of the Chinese cardinal points from those of Elam-Babylonia.—136. How they were changed during the migration.—137. The astronomical commands of Yas in the Shu-King suggests the same change.—138. The explanation is furnished by the palæographical derivation.—139. The same phenomenon explains a difficulty of the *Yh-king* with the Deluge legend.

IV.—§ 140. Ancient western traditions in old Chinese literature.—141. The Babylonian Animal-mother cosmogony in the Yh-King and in Lao-tze.—142. The sea-traders of the Erythræan sea arrived in 675 in Shantung, introduce coinage, astrology, and incite curiosity.—143. A search was then made for ancient documents, which studied by the Taoszeists were neglected by the Confucianists.

V.—§ 144. Stage of semi-hieroglyphism of the western writing borrowed by the Bak families.—145. The characters being old required explanations, whence the list of meanings in China as in the west.—146. Previous comparisons fully confirmed by further research.—147. A fuller list for *lu* and *li.*—148. It is a most conclusive proof.

VI.—§ 149. No pictorial writing in China before the Bak families.—150. Various causes of ideographical increase of their writing.

HISTORY AND METHOD.

On the 10th of May, 1880, at a special meeting of the Royal Asiatic Society, I presented a paper on the History of the Chinese Language, in which I communicated my discoveries on the old phonetic laws of spelling of the Ancient Chinese writing,—the derivation of this writing from the pre-cuneiform characters of South-Western Asia,—and also the nature and contents of the long-disputed book, the *Yh-King*. The printing of that paper was delayed in order to make it more precise and complete, but parts of its contents, as well as several results of my researches, had been published in 1880, by my friend Prof. R. K. Douglas and by myself.[1]

Since that time these results gained in accuracy and certainty,[2] and in January, 1882,[3] I was able to make

[1] See Prof. Douglas, *The Progress of Chinese Linguistic Discovery*, "The Times," April 20, 1880; reprinted in Trübner's *American, European, and Oriental Literary Record*, new series, vol. i. pp. 125-127, and my *China and the Chinese: their early history and future prospects*, in the *Journal of the Society of Arts*, July 16, 1880. *Early History of the Chinese Civilization* (with plate of old Chinese characters borrowed from the pre-cuneiform writing), London, 1880 (Trübner).

[2] Vid. an anonymous paper on *Chinese and Babylonian Literature* in *Quarterly Review* of July, 1882; and Prof. Douglas's charming volume on *China* (London, 1882, 8vo.). Vid. also the valuable report to the *Philological Society*, 1882, on *The Progress of Assyriology*, by Mr. T. G. Pinches.

[3] Published in *The Athenæum*, Jan. 21, 1882, as follows: "In company with the general body of Sinologists, I read with pleasure in your issue of the 7th your announcement that Dr. Legge's translation of the 'Yh King,' for the 'Sacred Books of the East' series, will be out about Easter. But the paragraph adds: 'Curiously enough, some Chinese scholars pretend that the book is written in the Accadian language.' As I was the first Sinologist to point out, two years ago, that the early Chinese civilization had been borrowed by the so-called Hundred families from the south of the Caspian Sea, I fear that the rather wild statement that the 'Yh King' was written in the Akkadian language may be confused with my own views, and I am, therefore, bound to protest against it. As the Chinese scholars, both English and Chinese, to whom I had occasion to

some important statements about the *Yh-King*, which bear in no inconsiderable manner on the origin and early history of Chinese culture.

submit my translation, attach, as I do myself, great importance to my discovery about the 'Yh King,' and as this discovery has caused so eminent a Sinologist as Prof. Douglas, of the British Museum, to join me in the preparation of a translation of the 'Yh King,' which we shall publish in English, and also in Chinese in China, it is important to state on what ground it stands.

It deals only with the oldest part of the book, the short lists of characters which follow each of the sixty-four headings of the chapters, and it leaves entirely aside the explanations and commentaries attributed to Wen Wang, Chöu Kung, Confucius, and others, from 1200 B.C. downwards, which are commonly embodied as an integral part of the classic. The proportion of the primitive text to these additions is about one-sixth of the whole. The contents of this primitive part of the book are not homogeneous, and belong to different periods of the early history of the Chinese. It has been made up to the number of sixty-four parts, to correspond with the speculations of numbers on the Kwa, at which time these old fragments and the mystical strokes have been joined together. To reach the sacred number of sixty-four it has been found advisable by the compiler to add texts much more recent than the older ones, of which the real meaning had been lost through the lapse of time and changes in the language. So different in subject are the various chapters that we find, for example, in several of them, curious ballads on historical or legendary events. In others we have descriptions of aboriginal tribes of China, their customs, the meanings of some of their words homonymous to the Chinese ones, instructions to the officials about them, and descriptions of the animals, which descriptions in the greatest number of cases are given in relation to their meanings of the character which is the subject of the chapter. Besides all this—and it is the most curious part of the book as well as the most special result of my discovery—we have a good number of chapters which are nothing else than mere lists of the meanings of the character placed at the head of the chapter. These lists are extraordinarily like the so-called syllabaries preserved in the Cuneiform characters, which were copied, as we know, by order of the Assyrian monarchs from older ones of Babylonia. The system of having such phonetic dictionaries with others of different kinds is a peculiar feature of the old Akkadian culture, on the mixed origin of which there is nothing here to say excepting this, that it was not carried bodily into Babylonia, but sprang up in that region from the intrusion of Northern peoples amongst the highly cultured Cushite populations, who had settled there and possessed that writing of hieroglyphic origin which became the Akkadian and later on the Cuneiform characters. Now there are many most serious facts which prove that writing and the elements of sciences, arts, and government were acquired in South-Western Asia by the future Chinese colonists from a centre of activity where the Babylonian or Akkadian culture had more or less directly been spread. It seems only natural, therefore, that the early Chinese leaders should have been induced, not only to keep some of the lists of values of the written characters which they had learned, but also to continue the some practice of making lists in relation to the peoples, customs, etc., of their new country. And though extraordinary, it is not astonishing that some of the oldest lists resemble the lists kept in the Cuneiform characters, and that I was able to exhibit two years ago at the Royal Asiatic Society four of those lists which run parallel in the 'Yh King' and in the Cuneiform texts. And no doubt the impossibility of reading, as current phrases and texts, simple lists of meanings accounts for the absolute obscurity of these parts of the book, and the astounding number of interpretations which have been proposed by native Chinese scholars. European scholars are engaged on the same path. We have already the Latin translation by P. Regis and others, made with the help of the Manchu version, which is quite unintelligible; the English translation of Canon McClatchie in the sense of a cosmogony; and the Latin translation in the 'Cursus Linguæ Sinicæ,' in course of publication at Shanghai, where is to be

Pending the publication of the version of this book I am preparing with the valuable help of Mr. Douglas, I have been advised, as it is a matter of much interest and importance, to put together some notes on the authorship[1] and history of the *Yh-King*, as well as on the scientific method of dealing with this, the oldest book of Chinese literature. Consequently I have classified my notes in the following order :

1. Description of the book.
2. Ancient texts on its authorship.
3. Influence of the evolution of writing.
4. Vestiges of the old text anterior to Wen Wang.
5. Native interpretations.
6. European interpretations.
7. Comparison of the interpretations.
8. Methods of interpretation.
9. Contents and origin of the *Yh-King*.

found one of the best translations of the Chinese classics which have ever been made. Besides these three, another translation in French is announced as being about to be published in the *Annales du Musée Guimet*, by M. E. Philastre, who for some years was a high official in Cochin China; this translation will exhibit a system of philosophy if we may judge from what the author has already written.

Dr. Legge's translation will certainly be an improvement upon the others already published. The many years of work which this Sinologist has spent upon it and his study of the commentaries will undoubtedly result in a great amount of information, as in his edition of some of the other Chinese classics.

So in a short time European scholars will have five translations of the 'Yh King' to compare, and when our translation, the sixth, appears, they will be able to decide which is the most faithful."

[1] Several misleading statements about the authorship and contents of this mysterious book, and the manner of translating it, have been lately published in an important place, *The Sacred Books of the East*, vol. xvi., the *Yî-King*, translated by J. Legge. The author has answered in his *Preface*, p. xix, rather sharply to the above letter of mine, and though he has made a *Yh-King* of his own fashion, having formulated the scheme supposed by some commentators more concisely than they have done (*Vid. ibid.* p. xiv), he dismisses the possibility of understanding the text of the book in a manner different from his own, for the reason that, according to his views and in his own words, "if you discard the explanations and commentaries attributed to King Wan, the Duke of Kaü, and Confucius, we take away the whole Yî. There remain only the linear figures attributed to Fû-hsi, without any lists of characters, long or short, without a single written character of any kind whatever." The proofs of the inaccuracy of these statements of Dr. Legge will be found throughout the following pages. His version has been thoroughly refuted by Prof. Douglas, in the *Academy* of July 12th, 1882, pp. 121-122, where is given a comparative version, according to our views, of the 30th chapter of the *Yh*. *Vid.* also my letters in the *Athenæum*, Sept. 9 and 30, 1882.

I. Description of the Book.

1. The *Yh-King* is the oldest of the Chinese books, and is the "*mysterious classic,*" which requires "*a prolonged attention to make it reveal its secrets*"; it has "*peculiarities of style, making it the most difficult of all the Chinese classics to present in an intelligible version.*"[1]

And the 1450 selected works on the *Yh-King* which are enumerated in the catalogue[2] of the great Library of the Emperor Kien-Lung, compiled in 1772–1790, point to anything but unanimity in the interpretation of the book by the Chinese themselves.[3]

"The 易經 *Yih King* 'Book of Changes,'" says the best of living Sinologists, Mr. A. Wylie, in his excellent *Notes on Chinese Literature*,[4] "is regarded with almost universal reverence, both on account of its antiquity, and also the unfathomable wisdom which is supposed to lie under its mysterious symbols. The authorship of these symbols 卦, which form the nucleus of the work, is with great confidence attributed to the ancient sage 伏犧 Fŭh he. These consisted originally of eight trigrams, but they were subsequently, by combining them in pairs, augmented to the number of sixty-four hexagrams."[5]

2. The figures or *Kwa* consist of six horizontal lines, divided or undivided,[6] placed one under the other. There is applied a special character to each hexagram, forming its name, at the beginning of each of the sixty-four chapters

---

[1] The italicised words are borrowed from Dr. Legge's *Preface*, in which we read also: "There is hardly another work in the ancient literature of China that presents the same difficulties to translate." See pp. xiii, xiv, xv.

[2] 欽定四庫全書總目. Cf. E. C. Bridgman, *Chinese Chrestomathy* (Macao, 1841, 4to.), p. xvii.

[3] The K'ang Hi's Imperial edition of the *Yh-King*, which appeared in 1715, contains quotations from the commentaries of 218 scholars, and these are (we take the words of Dr. Legge, *Introd.* p. 3) hardly a tenth of the men who have tried to interpret this remarkable book.

[4] The book opens with the *Yh-King*, the first of the classics, as do all the bibliographies, from the catalogue of the Han period downwards.

[5] See *Notes on Chinese Literature* (Shanghae, 1867, 4to.), p. 1.

[6] In the ordinary phraseology of the Yh, the lower one is called 貞; and the upper one 悔. The lines are: the 陽 *yang*, 剛 strong, 九 = 9, entire, undivided, and the 陰 *yn*, 柔 weak, 六 = 6, broken, divided.

composing the book. Each of these leading characters is followed by a certain number of others, and the entire chapter is arranged in seven lines under special headings, the first being the heading character, the other six an ordinal series, supposed to apply to each of the six lines of the hexagram individually, because their numbers are accompanied by the characters 九 or 六, indicating, in the opinion of the commentators, the undivided and divided lines. This set of characters, in seven divisions, the entire text in each chapter, is intermingled with fore-telling words—*lucky, unlucky, correct, no error*, etc.; but these divisions do not make as many phrases. The characters are disposed in little *sentences*, often of one character only, or of two or more. The meanings of these sentences are disconnected; they are quite independent one of the other, and do not bear openly on one same subject. A literal version of them is utterly unintelligible.[1] These peculiarities would place the *Yh-King* in an unexampled position if it were a book of continuous texts, as it has been hitherto wrongly thought to be by many discordant commentators and interpreters, as well Chinese as European.

3. The following commentaries are commonly printed with the text, as follows: The first (in 2 sections), with the heading 彖 *Twan*, disposed in two or more lines, is placed immediately after the first of the seven lines of the text. The second (in 2 sections), with the heading 象 *Siang*, is placed after the *Twan*, and after each of the following six lines of the text. Another one, the 文言 *Wen yen*, is annexed to the first two diagrams. All these compose the first and

---

[1] In a day of wisdom, a known Sinologist, Dr. Legge, in his version of the *Tso-chuen* (*Chin. Class.* vol. v. p. 169a), has made upon a quotation of the *Yh-King* this comment: "But it seems to me of no use trying to make out any principle of reason in passages like the present." *This view is the true one*, but we are sorry that the learned missionary, to whom we are indebted for a valuable though unequal version of several of the Chinese classics, has not stuck to it and refrained from publishing his paraphrase of the *Yh-King*. Speaking (The *Yi-King*, Pref. p. xv) of the literal Latin version done by PP. Regis, De Mailla, and Du Tartre, and also of his own first version, Dr. Legge writes: "But their version is all but unintelligible, and mine was not less so." However, Prof. Regis and his coadjutors had at their disposal all the help that Chinese lore could throw upon the *Yh*.

second Kiuen or books of the ordinary editions of the work.[1] A third Kiuen is composed of the following appendices: the 繫辭傳 *Hi-Tze Chuen* "Memoir on the Philosophy of the Text," in two sections; 說卦傳 *Shwoh Kwa chuen* "Discussion of the Diagrams"; 序卦傳 *Sü Kwa chuen* "The Order of the Diagrams"; and, finally, the 雜卦傳 *Tsa Kwa chuen* "Promiscuous Discourses on the Diagrams."

The *Twan*, the *Siang*, and the *Hi-tze*, being each divided into two sections,[2] all the appendices have received the name of "the Ten Wings" 十翼 of the *Yh-King*.

Such is, roughly described, this famous book as it has been handed down to the present time.

4. The *Twan* is commonly attributed to Wen Wang,[3] and the *Siang* to his son, Chöu Kung, in the twelfth century B.C., and there is no reason for throwing suspicion on this received tradition. The other "wings" are of different periods. In two of them, the *Hi-Tze* and the *Wen-yen*, is found repeatedly the same formula, 子曰 "The master said," as in the Confucian books, when the words of the great Sage are quoted; but this cannot be taken as a proof of date, even for these particular appendices, for, in one case at least, words and explanations from the *Wen-yen* are quoted[4] in history as early as 564 B.C., fourteen years before Confucius was born. Additions from the Sage's teachings have most likely been made afterwards to these appendices, apparently by one of

---

[1] Such as the 易經讀本 or 監本易經全文.

[2] In each, the first line of every chapter attributed to the entire diagram is considered as one part, called *Twan* or *Siang*, and the after lines as another part, called *Twan chuen* or *Siang chuen* respectively. The text is sometimes called 繫.

[3] Wen Wang 文王 "King Wen," or more properly the Elegant King, a posthumous title conferred by his son 丹 *Tan* 周公 *Chöu Kung*, the Duke of Chöu, to 昌 *Ch'ang*, the Chief of the West 西伯, father of 發 *Fa*, posthumously called *Wu Wang* 武王, the founder (1169-1116) of the Chöu dynasty. Wen Wang (1231-1135), for a state offence, was imprisoned at *Yu Li* 羑里, during two years (1144-1143), which he spent on the Yh-King. The 竹書紀年, of which the chronology down to 826 B.C. is different from the one commonly received, states that he remained six years in confinement.

[4] Cf. *Wen Yen*, 1st Kwa, §§ 1-3, and *Tso chuen*, Duke *Siang*, IXth year, § 3, in Legge's edition, p. 440.

his disciples, Shang Kiu, who is reputed to have handed down the *Yh* from his Master.

5. The wings and the text do not make a homogeneous work pervaded by the same ideas or produced by one mind. Their discrepancies and wide differences are not of the kind found between different pens dealing with and commenting on a plain text or a book of a known doctrine. They are not within the range of that mere variety of interpretation which occurs when several commentators have been treating of a recognized system commonly accepted. They lack that kind of unity of thought or of dealing with ideas which is the back-bone of commentaries, whatsoever they may be, and however wide may be their divergences of opinion; in fact, it seems that they are to be considered as attempts to understand the meaning of the book without knowing what it is. And this we see by the fact, that they introduce incongruous ideas, views, and systems of interpretation of their own. Certainly they have not been written at the same time as the text, nor at about the same period all together. Certain discrepancies of views can only have arisen by a not inconsiderable decay of the language during their respective compositions. Other discrepancies may be accounted for by a difference of dialectical spoken language, not of writing, between their authors. Some passages, for example, are but a mere enumeration of the different meanings of the temporary homonymous words with the sound of the heading character of each chapter. This process is followed in different ways. The author of the Wing called *Shwoh Kwa* 說卦, in his last section, has been very near finding the clue to the *Yh*. He has tried to explain the sound attached to the head-character of eight chapters (under the eight primitive *Kwas*). He gives lists of meanings for each of these sounds in homophonous words, according to his own pronunciation, which was no longer the same as that of the time when the early lists were compiled, and therefore, consequently, gives meanings which are not in the chapters.

6. The first two wings stand apart from the others, and exhibit more unity; at least more of that unity due to the repe-

tition of the same rows of characters, even when by an addition of some kind there is a sufficient clue to indicate that the text was differently understood. They have all the appearance of having been made to justify the arrangement of the text as they interpreted it, since they very often consist of a mere repetition of the text, frequently with slight modifications and differentiating additions. Their main characteristic is their obvious attempt to interpret the text in a symbolic sense, and to connect it with the linear composition of the hexagram at the head of each chapter, and with its lines individually. This is done plainly with more or less success by the *Siang*, which is divided accordingly. The *Twan* in a more general manner deals with the text as related to the hexagram as a whole, and to its strong and weak lines.

7. So much for the general contents of the ten wings. It is not my intention in any way to deal with them, but to leave them entirely aside, as far as my translation of the book goes. I was the first among Sinologists to disconnect openly the text from the appendices. For a scientific study of the contents of the text, and how it has been made, it is of absolute necessity to separate the commentaries from the text, and to treat of the latter alone. The whole book, text and wings, contains 24,107 characters; the text alone, in its 450 lines (from 2 to 30 characters), has 4134 characters only, or about one-sixth of the whole.

II. THE AUTHORSHIP OF THE BOOK.

8. Though Chinese literature is not without several indications as to some authors of the *Yh-King*, and echoes of old traditions collected by independent scholars, there is not, in the modern statements, that unity of views which would afford a satisfactory basis for investigation. The reason of this is obvious. The names of Fuh-hi, Wen Wang, and Confucius, form so sacred a Trinity, that the mere fact of their having been each more or less connected with the making of the book as it now stands, has prevented many writers from quoting any tradition which would have detracted from the

glory of either of the three as a sharer in the authorship of the work; hence, they were contented to say, in a general way, that the book was the work of the three saints, attributing the _Kwas to_ Fuh-hi, the text to Wen Wang, and the appendices to Confucius, a statement the slightest criticism would have easily exploded and shown to be ridiculous and against evidence.

9. We find for example only in popular or unscholarly books, as the 歷代帝王年表,¹ such statements as these:

"Tai Hao Fuh hi begins to delineate the eight Kwas 太皡 伏羲始畫八卦."²

"Chöu Sin 11th year 紂辛十一祀 (*i.e.* 1144 B.C.) confines Si Pöh at Yu-Li 囚西伯於羑里. Si Pöh practises the Yh 西伯演易." And at the end of this very last reign of the Yn dynasty, we find another entry: "*The* Yh has text to the sixty-four Kwas 易有六十四卦辭."

And at the end of the entries relating to the events of the reign of Ching Wang 成王, we read:

"The Yh has text to the three hundred and eighty-four lines 易有三百八十四爻辭."

And, finally, in King Wang, 36th year: "敬王三十六年, Kung tze makes *the* ten wings of the Yh 孔子作易十翼."

10. But if we turn to more scholarly and ancient texts, we find different, in some cases very precise, statements. They, however, almost all agree in their attribution of the invention of the Kwas to the first name which appears at the dawn of their traditions with an appearance of personality, Fuh-hi.

Here are a few extracts about this first point:

(*a*) "In accordance with the Tortoise writings 應之龜書, Fuh-hi imitating their figures 伏犧乃則象, made the Kwas of the Yh 作易卦."³

---

¹ *Li Tai Wang nien piao*, p. 5.
² *Tai Hao* = 'great whitish,' also the 'western region':—*Fuh-hi*, also written in different manners 庖犧, 密犧, 宓戲, 虙戲.
³ 禮含文嘉, in *Tai Ping yü lan*, K. 78, f. 3.

(b) "Fuh-hi imitated the Tortoise writing 伏羲則龜書, and made the eight Kwas 乃作八卦."[1]

(c) "Pao-hi made the eight Kwas 庖犧氏作而八卦, and arranged their lines 列其蓍. Hien Yuen arose 軒轅氏興, and the Tortoise and the Divining stalks exhibited their varieties 而龜策彰其彩."[2]

(d) "Pao-hi drew the Kwas 庖犧畫卦, in order to establish their symbolism 以立象. Hien Yuen began the characters 軒轅氏造字, in order to set up their instructions 以設教."[3]

It is useless to continue these quotations repeating the same thing over and over again, inasmuch as one of the commentaries of the Yh, the *Hi-tze*, second part, first section, gives the same statement:

(e) "Pao-hi first made the eight Kwas 庖犧...始作八卦."

11. So much for the first delineation of the eight Kwas. As to their multiplication, the unanimity of the traditions ceases, though the larger number of them attribute the operation to Shen-nung.

In the *San Hwang pön Ki* 三皇本紀, compiled by Se-ma Cheng 司馬貞 during the eighth century, the famous commentator of Se-ma Tsien's 司馬遷 *She Ke* 史記, and generally printed at the beginning of this celebrated history, we find[4] the same statement about Fuh-hi, and about Shen-nung[5] we read:

(f) "He blended the *Yh*, and returned each to its place, 交易而退各得其所. Afterwards he multiplied the eight Kwas into 64 diagrams 遂重八卦爲六十四爻."

And in the *Ti Wang She Ki*,[6] quoted again at *h*, we read:

(g) "Shen-nung multiplied the numbers of the eight Kwas 重八卦之數, carried them to the square of eight 究八八之體, and formed the 64 Kwas 爲六十四卦."

---

[1] 字學典, f. 34, in the great Cyclopedia in 10,000 Kiuen, *Kin ting Ku Kin t'u shu tsih cheng*.
[2] 魏書江式傳.   [3] 張懷瓘書斷.
[4] *Vid.* f. 1 v. and f. 3.   [5] Shen-nung, 2737-2697 B.C.?
[6] *Vid. Tai Ping Yü Lan*, K. 78, f. 5 v. *Vid.* n. 3, following page.

In the above quoted wing of the *Yh*,[1] progress of arts and inventions are attributed to the contemplation of several hexagrams (thirteen in number), which in nine cases at least [2] cannot be confused with the trigrams, and as these inventions are, several of them, connected with Shen-nung, etc., we see that, in the opinion of the time of the writer, most likely anterior to Confucius for that part, at least, the multiplication of the Kwas was *un fait accompli* at the earliest period.

12. In a most valuable Cyclopedia in 1000 kiuen, compiled in 977–983, the *Tai Ping yü Lan*,[3] we read:—

(*h*) "The *Chronicle of Emperors and Kings* (by Hwang P'u Mih, a celebrated scholar of the third century, A.D. 215–282) says: 帝王世紀曰 The Pao-hi made the eight Kwas; 庖羲氏作八卦. Shen-nung multiplied them into sixty-four Kwas; 神農重之爲六十四卦 Hwang-Ti Yao and Shun 黃帝堯舜 developed the hint 引而伸之, and divided it into two Yhs 分爲二易; down to the men of the Hia *dynasty* 至夏人, who called *one* on account of Yen-Ti[4] *Lien Shan* 因炎帝曰連山, and the men of the Yn dynasty who called *the other* on account of Hwang-Ti *Kwei-Tsang*[5] 殷人因黃帝曰歸藏. Wen Wang enlarged the sixty-four Kwas 文王廣六十四卦, made clear the lines 9 and 6 著九六之爻, and denominated it the Yh of Chöu 謂之周易."

13. In one of the best critical parts of the *Lu she* 路史,[6] by Lo Pi 羅泌, of the Sung Period, we read:

---

[1] 繫辭, 2nd part, ch. ii.
[2] 16, 17, 21, 34, 38, 42, 43, 59, 62.
[3] 太平御覽 K. 609, f. 2. A very interesting notice of this Cyclopedia, and its adventures since its compilation, is given by Mr. A. Wylie, *Notes on Chinese Literature*, pp. 146, 147. On Hwang P'u Mih, vid. Dr. Legge's *Prolegomena* to the *Shu-King*, p. 26; and also Mayer's *Chinese Reader's Manual*, n. 216.
[4] *Yen-Ti = Shen-nung.*
[5] The *Lien-shan* is said to have included eight myriads of words, and the *Kwei-tsang* 4300. I shall discuss this tradition and its bearing when tracing the history of the written text of the *Yh*, and shall quote a traditional list of the headings of chapters which have been modified by Wen Wang. *Vid.* § 31.
[6] 路史餘論, Kiuen 2, f. 1. In Wylie's *Notes on Chinese Literature*, p. 24, is the following appreciation of the work:—"The historical portion is considered of little value, and the author seems to have been led astray by an undue attachment to Taouist legends, but there is a good deal of learning shown in the geographical and critical parts" (here quoted).

(i) "In his time Fuh-hi 伏羲之時 himself multiplied the eight Kwas 入卦自重, and himself discoursed upon them and distributed for use 亦自詳于施用; but this text has no place in literature 特末見之文字. Arriving at the *Lien-Shan* and *Kwei-Tsang* 至連山與歸藏, the upper and lower divisions of the *Yh* 反易上下 and the illustrations of the hexagrams were all completed 則爻象巳大備, but in that age they were not deeply studied 而世弗深究. Coming down to the time of Wen Wang 降及文王, while imprisoned at Yu-Li 拘囚羑里 he used them for divination 用以卜筮. He added and surreptitiously introduced the foretelling words 加竄繇辭, and he altered the inferring numbers 更改衍數, in order to regulate the divining stalks of the Great Inference 以立大衍之策, that those using them could draw the inference 更之可衍. And afterwards the arguments began to be discoursed upon 而後文辭始詳. In consequence it was called the Yh of Chöu 遂名之以周易."

This disquisition on the early history of the *Yh* is most important, and seems to have been done with great care; it throws light on some passages of ancient authors I shall have to quote, which otherwise would not seem to require so precise a translation as it is necessary to make, in order to understand them without contradictions. It displays an amount of critical research most praiseworthy. The translation of the passage just given can be entirely trusted, as it is not only the joint work of Prof. Douglas and myself, but has also been revised by an eminent native Chinese scholar. I shall, later, have to deal with what is said about the text previous to the Chöu dynasty, as well as with other information given later in the same work, but with this I have nothing to do in the present stage of my investigations.

14. I will now turn to some older texts bearing upon part of the work done by Wen Wang.

And here I find two allusions to it almost in the same terms in the longest wing of the *Yh*,[1] from which we have already

---

[1] *Hi-tze*, part ii. ch. 7 and 11.

twice borrowed some information. There we read, in Dr. Legge's translation:

(*j*) "Was it not in the middle period of antiquity[1] that the Yh began to flourish? Was not he who made it (or were not they who made it) familiar with anxiety and calamity?" And in another passage:

(*k*) "Was it not in the last age of the Yn (dynasty), when the virtue of Chöu reached its highest point, and during the troubles between Wen Wang and (the tyrant) Chöu, that (the study of) the Yh began to flourish?"

This *does not* say that Wen Wang wrote the text of the book, but only that its study began to flourish in his time. We know by other traditions that its study was neglected before, and all this agrees perfectly well. However, as Wen Wang had a great deal to do with this study, we can only take the tradition about his pretended authorship of the text as a summary statement, avoiding complicated explanations, the more so that this is in complete agreement with the nature of the Chinese, whose veneration for the ancestors of their statutes concentrates everything on the star-men of their night-like historical traditions.

15. From the third commentary of the *Yh*, I have now to come down to the second century B.C., and must consult the celebrated *Historical Records* 史紀 of the Herodotus of China, Se-ma Tsien 司馬遷. In his *Chöu Pön Ki* 周本紀, a certain passage added to the life of *Si Pöh* = Wen Wang (which has all the appearance of an interpolation), I read:[2]

(*l*) "When he was imprisoned at *Yu-Li* 北囚癸里, he (Wen Wang) extended 蓋 the profitable changes 益易 proper to the eight Kwas 之入卦[3] in favour of the sixty-four Kwas 爲六十卦."

---

[1] The period of middle antiquity, according to Chinese commentators, begins with the rise of the Chöu in the twelfth century B.C., and it finishes at the Confucian Era. But we are not sure that this explanation has not been made up for the occasion of this passage.

[2] See *Kiuen* 4, f. 5 v.

[3] It seems to me that we cannot translate here, otherwise than considering 之 as having its meaning = 於; else the phrase would be in contradiction with the facts certainly known to Se-ma Tsien and his father, of the multiplication of the

It is here plainly indicated, as in the quotations above (*h*, *i*), the very work of Wen Wang, who, distinguishing the weak and strong lines, has extended their eight changes so as to correspond with the text.

16. In the *Former Han Records*, compiled by Pan Ku, some one hundred and fifty years after the *Historical Records* of Se-ma Tsien, I read in the section on *Literature*:[1]

(*m*) "Wen Wang then multiplied the six lines (of transformation) of the Yh 文王於是重易六爻, and made the first and second book 作上下篇. Kung She formed with the Yh's 孔氏為之 *Twan, Siang, Hi tze, Wen yen, Sü Kwa*, the ten supplementary books 彖象繫辭文言序卦之屬十篇."

This is in perfect agreement, excepting the substitution of the *Sü Kwa* for the *Shwoh Kwa*, with what had been said before by Se-ma Tsien, who, in his "Life of Confucius,"[2] had written:

(*n*) "Kung tze, when old, also enjoyed the Yh 孔子晚而喜易. He arranged (or put in order[3]) 序 the *Twan*, the *Hi*, the *Siang*, the *Shwoh Kwa*, and the *Wen yen* 彖繫象說卦文言.[4] During his study, the leather thong of (his copy of) the Yh was thrice worn out 讀易韋編三絕."

17. This is all that is said by Se-ma Tsien, and nothing more, and it is this passage which has been quoted[5] as the proof that, according to Se-ma Tsien, Confucius wrote several appendixes to the Yh. As a matter of fact, the great Historian says nothing of the kind, and to what extent the pencil of Confucius has been at work in the Appendices is entirely left in the dark by the historical quotations which have been found about it.

Kwas before the time of Wen Wang. For this manner of translating 之 see Julien, *Syntaxe nouvelle*, vol. i. p. 159, and Legge's *Chinese Classics*, passim. If my translation of this phrase were not the right one, how is it that Pan Ku has not repeated the same thing, but gives a statement which is much more in accordance with my translation? However, it is rather unsatisfactory.

[1] *Vid.* 前漢書, Kiuen 30, f. 2.
[2] *Vid. She Ki*, K. 47, *Kung tze She Kia*, f. 24 v.
[3] For the use of the same word with the same meaning in the same chapter, see *ibid*, f. 23 v.
[4] These, with the 序卦 and 雜卦, are all the appendixes of the *Yh*.
[5] Dr. Legge, *Yi King*, Introd. p. 26.

The absolute silence about the work of Chöu Kung, if the *Siang* 象 comes from his pen, would be worth considering, if there was not elsewhere (in the *Tso chuen*) a recognition of his authorship. The text is speaking of an envoy of the Marquess of Tsin to the State of Lu.[1]

(o) "Looking at the books in charge of the great historiographer 觀書於大史氏, he saw the Siang of the Yh and the Chun Tsiu of Lu 見易象與魯春秋, and said: 曰 the uttermost of the Institutes of Chöu are in Lu 周禮盡在魯矣. Now, indeed I know the virtues of the Duke of Chöu, 吾乃今知周公之德, and how the Chöu attained to Royalty, 與周之所以王也."

This happened in 540 B.C., when Confucius was yet a child of eleven years, and so, some sixty years before he enjoyed the *Yh King*.

18. Besides the indications to be found in the historical texts and traditions set forth in the preceding pages, there is much valuable information as to the earlier *Yh*, and the progress of the *Yh* of Chöu from 672 to 486 B.C. in this same *Tso-chuen*, supplement by Tso k'iu Ming to the *Ch'un Tsiu* of Lu, compiled by Confucius.

The Kwas and their appended meanings and list of characters are quoted some twenty times in the *Tso-chuen*. Studying these with care they give the most suggestive information as to the history and composition of the book.

19. I resume these quotations as follows: 22nd year of Duke Chwang (672): The Yh of Chöu brought and consulted in the state of Ch'in by an officer of Chöu. The same thing happens in the 7th year of Duke Süen (602).

The milfoil consulted in Tsin, Tsi, Ts'in, Lu States in 1st and 2nd years of Duke Min (661–660); three times in 15th year of Duke Hi (645); 25th year of Duke Hi (635); 16th year of Duke Ch'ing (575); 9th year of Duke Siang (564); 25th year same duke (548).

---

[1] *Tso Chuen*, Duke Ch'ao, 2nd year. Legge edit. p. 583, translates :—"When he looked at the (*various*) documents in the charge of the great historiographer, and the Ch'un Ts'iew of Loo, he said, 'The institutes of Chow are all in Loo. Now, indeed, I know the virtue of the Duke of Chow, and how it was that (the House of) Chow attained to the Royal dignity.'"

The Yh of Chöu consulted in Tsin, Lu, Ts'in, Wei States: 12th year of Duke Süen (597); 9th year of Duke Siang (564); 28th year of same Duke (545); 1st, 5th, 7th, 12th, 29th, 32nd years of Duke Chao (541, 537, 535, 530, 513, 509); 9th year of Duke Ngai (486 B.C.).

The Yh of Chöu does not appear in the Tsin state before 597, in Lu before 564, in Tsi before 548, etc., and before these dates, in 672 and 602, only in the hands of officers of Chöu. The milfoil, however, was often consulted in the same states before these dates, and some texts more or less alike to Chöu's Yh text are quoted.

20. The result appears to be that the *Yh* of Chöu was more especially used in the state of Chöu than elsewhere, but was not in common use in the other states so early as 672, though the book existed at the time. In this year the great Historiographer of Chöu uses himself the Yh of Chöu, of which he had brought a copy with him, in the state of 陳 Ch'in, and quotes the exact characters of Kwa xx. 6–4, of the present text of the book. Afterwards we do not find the Yh of Chöu quoted till 70 years after this first date, and once again, in the state of Ch'in, by an officer of Chöu, who quotes a meaning. In the mean time, not less than six times, the divining milfoil is consulted in the states of Tsi, Tsin and Ts'in; hexagrams are quoted, meanings and text are reproduced, exhibiting discrepancies with the present text, and in any case never extracted from the *Siang*.

21. After the occurrence in 602 above quoted, the *Yh* of Chow is again consulted in 597 in the state of Tsin, and, excepting two occasions in 575 in Tsin, and 548 in Tsi, when "divining by the milfoil" is the expression used, there occur in the records of the years 564, 545, 541, 537, 535, 512, 509, and 486 extracts which are all exact quotations of the *Yh* of Chöu, being meanings and characters from the text or the *Siang*, though not always in accord with Dr. Legge's translation. In 564, the foretelling words of the *Yh* of Chöu are distinctly quoted *in addition to the meaning of the Kwa quoted from the older Yh*, and in 540, when Confucius was a child of eleven years, the Archives of the state of Lu are congratulated for containing

the Siang of the *Yh* by the Duke of Chöu, as we have seen above.

All this points unmistakably to the existence of the text of the *Yh* as independent and anterior to the *Yh* of Chöu.[1] When this last is not *eo nomine* quoted, and when they only say that they divine by the milfoil, they never quote any passage from the Siang, but only characters and meanings of the text.

22. I do not find in any ancient authority, the assertion so simple in itself, that. Wen Wang did or wrote the *text of the Yh*. It has crept out as the expression of a natural Chinese feeling, and is to be found only in rather recent time. Even as late as the twelfth century, the *Chöu yh pön ngi* 周易本義, by the famous Chu Hi 朱熹, does not express it.[2] It is a mistake to believe in a common consensus or general and unique tradition attributing the authorship of the *text of the Yh* to this king and his son, and all those who may follow what has been stated lately with great emphasis by a well-known Sinologist will only repeat a serious error. And the mistake will be the more amusing if, as has been done, they appeal to the traditions and beliefs of foreigners; it is difficult to know what may be the traditions and beliefs of foreigners about the *Yh*, as they cannot have any others than those they have picked up in some Chinese books. At any rate they may be dismissed at once by inquirers as second-hand information,[3] as until now the matter has never been seriously investigated.

[1] One of the most striking passages from the *Tso-chuen*, justifying all that we have stated, is the quotation said to be from the 18th Kwa 蠱, and in which are quoted meanings borrowed from the 40th Kwa 解, in different order and with serious discrepancies of characters. This occurs during the fifteenth year of Duke Hi, and is not quoted as from the *Yh* of Chöu. It comes obviously from the older text, previously to its arrangement by Wen Wang.

[2] He says (according to the 南海縣志藝文, k. xxv. f. 2 v.): "Fuh-hi made the 64 Kwas 伏羲作六十四卦; Chöu Kung connected the words of the lines 周公係爻辭 with the main emblems 與夫象, the prognostics 占, the Kwas 卦, and the series of their mutations and explanations 變之說之類是也."

[3] However, we shall be contented to quote one of the best European Sinologists who mentions the primitive text of the Yh. "According to the Chinese belief,

The comparison of all these authorities of different periods makes it clear, without possible doubt, to any unprejudiced mind, *that the text of the Yh existed long before Wen Wang,*[1] though not exactly as it now stands; that he studied it, modified it, and commented upon it.[2]

III.—INFLUENCE OF THE EVOLUTION OF WRITING.

23. The remarkable evolution of speech and of writing in China, their early association and close connexion, their subsequent dissociation and respective disintegration,[3] are of prime importance for any scientific investigation of the oldest texts of Chinese literature. We have multifarious proofs that the writing, first known in China, was already an old one,[4] partially decayed, but also much improved since

---

these eight figures (the eight Kwas), together with the sixty-four combinations to which they are extended, accompanied by certain presumptive explanations attributed to Fuh-hi, were the basis of an ancient system of philosophy and divination during the centuries preceding the era of Wen Wang . . ." See Mayer's *Chinese Reader's Manual*, vol. ii. p. 241, who quotes (p. 336) his native authorities, none of which have been quoted above, and consequently are to be added to them.

[1] In a dictionary of the Han period, the 釋名 by 劉熙 (2nd cent. A.D. ?) we read that "At the time of the Canon of Yao 唯堯典 (2356-2255 B.C. ? or 2145-2042 B.C. ?) *they kept the Yh* 存易.

[2] There are several passages in the text of the Yh which have been interpreted as allusions to places or facts connected with the rising of the Chöu, etc., but this is not the place to deal with them. It will be seen in my translation or scientific analysis of the text, that they have nothing to do with the meanings which have been forced upon them afterwards.

[3] For want of space, I have to summarize in this section a score of pages in which I had summed up from my large work in preparation on the subject the leading facts and proofs of this double evolution.

[4] We have convincing proofs (vid. my *Early History*, pp. 21-23, and the last section of the present paper) that it had been borrowed, by the early leaders of the Chinese Bak families (Pŭh Sing) in Western Asia, from an horizontal writing traced from left to right, the pre-cuneiform character, which previously had itself undergone several important modifications. Following their old habit of notched sticks and knotted cords, the Chinese disposed in perpendicular lines, and consequently had to put up the characters too wide for the regularity of the columns. This was done according to the objects represented by the characters. Vid. for example the Ku-wan shapes of the following characters: turned up: 口, the two lips and tip of the tongue = mouth ; 曰, the two lips open and breath = speak ; 甘, the two lips and something in the mouth = taste ; 目, = the eye, etc., etc. Turned up from the left : 言, the two lips open and voice = speech ; 𨸏, two heights = colline ; 龜 = a tortoise ; 馬, an animal, afterwards a horse ; etc., etc. Turned up from the right : 舟 = a boat ; 臣, the upper part

its primitive hieroglyphic stage. Although many of them had kept their early pictographic and ideographic values, the characters, selected according to their sense were used phonetically,[1] isolated and in groups, to represent the monosyllabic and polysyllabic words, as well as the compounds[2] of the spoken

---

of the face = minister; 臣, the lower part of the face, the chin; 頁, a seated man, good; etc., etc.

[1] The phonetic combinations in early Chinese have been singularly disturbed by the putting up spoken of in the last note. In the borrowed compounds, when unchanged in direction, the reading goes from left to right; when put up from the left, it reads from top to bottom; when put up from the right, the most frequent, it reads from bottom to top. These various directions, according to the shape, size, and sense of the characters, were imitated afterwards in the new compounds, as long as and where the old principles of phonetic orthography were not forgotten. Here are a few examples of this orthography in the oldest Chinese characters transcribed in modern style of writing: 南 = *Nam* (mod. *Nan*) was written with 羊 = *Nen* (mod. *Jen*) under 木 = *Muh*; 去 = *Kop* (mod. *Kü*) was written 凵 = *Kam* (mod. *K'an*) under 父 = *Ping*; 先 = *Din* (mod. *Sien*) was written 之 = *Dik* (mod. *Chi*) over 人 = *Nen* (mod. *Jen*); 仙 = *Sen* (mod. *Sien*) was written 山 = *San* (mod. *Shan*) followed on the right by 人 = *Nen*; 耿 = *Keng* was written 火 = *Kwo* followed on the right by 耳 = *Nip* (mod. *Œt*); 仁 = *Jen* was written 尸 = *Shi* followed on the right by 二 = *Ni* (mod. *Œt*); etc., etc.

[2] The orthography of the bisyllabic or polysyllabic words presents the same phenomena of reading as the two-consonanted words, and for the same reasons. The only disturbing fact which may prevent their recognition is that, the final of the second syllable having been often dropped by phonetic decay, the compound has the appearance of a biconsonanted word. The reading most frequently found for these compounds is generally from left to right, but the other directions also occur. The great interest in this discovery is that the old groups did express not only the monoconsonant- or biconsonant syllables, but also the polysyllables and compound words of the colloquial, many of which can still be recognized, though more or less decayed since that time. In the comparison with the spoken words, it is important not to forget that the characters used to express the compound words in colloquial are not to be pressed by themselves as a help to restore the older sound of the expression, as they have been used only afterwards to express the spoken word, and they are not etymologically connected to it. The book-language of the dialects is more fallacious than useful for this purpose. A few examples of various kinds are necessary to illustrate these explanations. Ex. 摶 *tw'an* = to roll up, to beat, was written in Ku-wen 支干矛 and 支干每 which both read *TKM*, as the three characters were *Tih* (mod. *chi*), *Kan*, and *Meu* or *Muh*. Now the colloquial has kept an expression 打滾 = *ta kwan* = 'to roll about on the ground,' which is obviously the same with a slight differentiation of meaning, whilst the phonetic decay in the older official dialect has contracted the whole together into *tw'an*. Ex. 咸 = *hien* = 'all, the whole of,' was written in the Ku-wen 廿 = *Kam* under 戌 = *Thu*, or *Kam-thu*, for which we find the colloquial *hien-tsih* (咸 集) and the contracted form *kat* (皆 mod. *kiai*). Ex. 斕 = *Lan* in Ku-wen 文粦 = *Ban-Lan* (mod. *Wen-lan*), and in colloquial *Pan-lan* 文扁 斕 = 'variegated colours.' 禱 = *Tao* = 'to pray,' in Ku-wen same orthography: 示 = *Ki* + 壽 = *Tho*, in colloquial 祈 禱 = *K'i-tao* or

language.¹ At that time the writing of the *Ku-wen* was really the phonetic expression of speech.² (By an analysis of the old inscriptions and fragments, and by the help of the

告 禱 *Kao-tao*, the contracted form is *Kit* 祈 mod. *K'i*, etc. etc. *Vid.* other examples below, § 31, and the following note.

To understand, with this true history of the Chinese characters, the rough hieroglyphic signs which (more or less exactly reproduced in every European book treating of the writing) are wrongly quoted as primitive, and present a striking contrast to the really advanced state of the oldest written words, we must not forget, besides the hieroglyphical revival of 820 B.C. (which has produced no inconsiderable influence on the pictography of the characters), that these rough signs are found only on made-up antiquities, or misunderstood imitations, and also in rude inscriptions written by men unacquainted with the science of writing, which was the privilege only of a small number of the learned. We have in the *Tso-chuen* many proofs of this last assertion, as the 'Book of Odes' could be read or sung intelligibly only by specialists.

¹ The Chinese languages are phonetically decayed in the extreme; however, in their present stage they are not monosyllabic, but agglutinative. The theory of their monosyllabism, and in fact its sad influence on linguistic progress, arose from a misunderstanding of the syllabism of the present writing supposed to be spoken, and the wrong assimilation of the old writing to it; and also from the confusion between the monosyllabisms of elocution and of decay, with a supposed logical monosyllabism; the whole combined with the false hypothesis of a primeval monosyllabism.

² Here is an interesting proof of this remarkable fact, from the *Shu-king*, *The great announcement*, 大誥, § 2. The *Ku-wen* phrase is from the text engraved on stone (245 A.D.) in three styles, *Ku-wen*, *Siao-chuen*, and *Li-shu* (Vid. 三字石經, f. 6). The phrase we take as an example is in modern style: 越玆蠢, translated by Medhurst, 'And now we see their stupid commotions,' and by Dr. Legge, 'Accordingly we have the present senseless movements,' This supposed despising expression is intended to qualify a military rising, which had been prognosticated in the West according to the preceding phrase. But as the troubles arose in the East, there is a disagreement which the commentators childishly solve by saying that the troubles arose indeed in the East, but they necessarily went on to trouble the West. The Ku-wen text gives the solution of the difficulty, which came from an inaccuracy of the transcribers. It reads as follows: 粵玆戩 = *Yueh tze chun*, which in spoken language cannot be understood, but which disintegrated as we must do for the Ku-wen, give: 于閑玆春戈 = *yü-shen tze chun-ko*, are more audible and completely intelligible to the ear in the colloquial *yu-shen tze tung-ko* 尤甚玆動戈 = *moreover (is) this rising-in-arms*. The above quoted translation must be amended according to the latter, which is the true meaning of the genuine text; it does not imply any contradiction, as the modern text does; the king alludes here obviously to the actual outbreak in the East, and not at all to the predicted troubles in the West. As to the necessary philological apparatus of this reading, which I shall give in my *Outlines of the Evolution of Speech and Script in China*, it will be sufficient to say that: 春 *ch'un* was formerly *tün*; 粵 =*vu-than* (mod. *yu-shen*) contracted in the compounds in *viet* (Sin-Ann.) *yueh* (Mand.), is still found under the false written etymology 粵省 (*Viet-tinh*) *yüeh-sheng*, a name for the Canton province. I hope that direct proofs, as this example from the Shu-king, will convince the Sinologists of the truth of my discovery of the reading of the old Chinese texts, and consequently, how important it is to gather all that remains still to be found in China of texts in ancient or Ku-wen characters.

native works on palæography (some most valuable), I have compiled a dictionary of this period.) But such a writing could not last long, as gradually and inequally the old principles of orthography were lost, while this orthography was not modified to follow the evolution of the spoken language, and the segregation of dialects parallel with the territorial expansion of Chinese culture and power. In fact, the groups were gradually considered as mere ideograms, and the discrepancies which arose in the various states of the Chinese agglomeration rendered necessary some kind of unification.

24. This task was attempted, at a moment of temporary revival of power of the Chöu dynasty, under Süen Wang, by his great historiographer She Chöu. This great minister undertook, about 820 B.C., to modify the writing in such a manner that it could be understood whatever might be the dialectical differences between the states. For this purpose he drew up his *Ta-chuen* style; rectifying the characters pictographically, restoring many hieroglyphic shapes according to his views, and adding ideographic characters to many existing and known groups in order to give the necessary precision and to avoid any misunderstanding.[1] He tried to speak to the eye and no longer to the ear.[2] In

---

[1] I have also compiled a vocabulary of this writing, of which the principles afterwards imitated have been so powerful a factor in the mental and political history of Chinese culture.

[2] The survival of pictography and hieroglyphism, which She-chöu gave to the writing by his modifications of the characters, can be fully illustrated by the two following examples. The phonetic group for 'wild country,' 'desert,' 野, was written in Ku-wen 埜 = 土 *Tu* 'earth,' under 林 *Lam*, mod. *lin*, 'forest,' *i.e.* *T* initial under *L* final, to be read *T—L*, which we find still in the Corean *tel* and in the decayed Sinico-Annamite *da*. This was all right so long as the reading was not forgotten and the colloquial remained unaltered. But when and where this agreement break up, the ideographical value of the combination, deprived of its phonetic reading, in the regions where had begun the phonetic decay which has turned gradually the primitive *tel* into the modern *ye*, was no more suggestive enough of the intended solitude. *She-chöu* for the purpose of suggesting this savageness added the ideograph for *isolate* (not *spear*) into the group, and wrote it 埜 (not 埜). The proof of the early bisyllabism *T-L* of this word is very likely to be seen in the colloquial *ye-lu* (野 路), *ye* decayed of *te*. Again, the group 葬 'to bury,' 'to conceal,' was not sufficiently expressive to the eyes; the historiographer of Chöu in framing anew the character substituted 葬 to its central part 死 in order to suggest 'hidden in the ground as reptiles do,' and did not consider the phonetic expression, which was entirely thrown over by him.

the states where his very characters were not used, his principles of ideographism at least were extensively followed, though not accepted everywhere.[1] The decline of the Middle-Kingdom let the matter drift again.

25. When Ts'in She Hwang Ti brought all the states under his sway, one of his first cares was to have an uniform writing in the empire. He had, about 227 B.C., the *Siao Chuen* framed by a simplification of the *Ta Chuen* of Se-Chöu on the same principles, according to a previously fixed standard of various strokes,[2] and, a few years afterwards, the *Li Shu*, more square, and fitted to the use of the pencil, newly improved. From the time of She-Chöu, the system of ideographic *aphones* had facilitated the use of added characters as phonetics to express new sounds and new meanings;[3] this process of ideo-phonetic groups was largely used in the new writings, and became the principal factor in the writing of new words from that time downwards. In their otherwise rather childish explanation of the old formula of the *Luh Shu*, the Han scholars had recognized the importance of this process. Finally, about 350 A.D., the celebrated caligrapher Wang Hi Che, without modifying the principles, gave to the writing the modern pattern the *Kiai Shu*, which, excepting a slight improvement during the Sung period, is still in general use.[4]

[1] And so was established officially, for political reasons, the wide gap which separates the written style from the spoken language; a difficulty of which the solution gives the link of the respective evolution of speech and writing in China.

[2] The deformation undergone by the old characters (in the cases of no substitution) when transcribed with the small canons of fixedly shaped strokes of the *Li-shu*, *Siao-chuen*, and finally modern style *Kiai-shu*, is the great difficulty which the palæographer has to overcome. It complicates singularly the graphical etymologies by apparent, but in reality false, similarities, too often accepted as genuine by many uncritical Chinese historians of their writing. The same complication presents itself to those who study the history of the Cuneiform characters.

[3] The ideographic determinatives *aphone* began since that time to be more and more extensively used; before She-Chöu the process had only been initiated in a few places. At first, at least in some quarters, in order to show their non-phonetic value, they were written smaller and rather under the character or group which they were intended to determinate. Cf. for the determinatives 叉, 口, 攵, 亻, 禾, 貝, 辵, in the inscriptions of which the facsimile are published in the palæographical collection of Yuen Yuen, 積古齋鐘鼎彝器款諸, K. iv. ff. 36-39.

[4] The influence of the advanced civilization and the mixture of the Ougro-Altaïc early Chinese immigrants with the native populations of China of several states (of which the primitive Taï or Shan was not the least important) were not

26. The evolution of the Chinese writing being not only a matter of form and shape, but a matter of principles, it would be childish to suppose that the character of the old texts could be found in the modern characters, allowing even for the necessary modification in the shape of the strokes. It does not require any explanation to understand that any text to be transcribed from the early *Ku-wen* into *Ta-chuen*, next into *Siao-chuen* or *Li-shu*, afterwards in *Kiai-shu* styles, ought to have been thoroughly clear to the scribes, even supposing that the latter had always been earnest and unprejudiced writers. But what in the case of unintelligible texts? Exactly what has happened to the *Yh-King*. The purpose of the transcribers being only the ideographical confined to the area of their political power. This deep mixture which has produced the Chinese physical type and peculiar speech, and accounts for several phonetic features common to the Chinese and many Indo-Chinese languages, as well as for the reciprocal loan of words, which amounts between the Chinese and Taï vocabularies to more than 30 per cent, had begun outside long before the extension of the Chinese political supremacy. And as to this extension, I may remark that the publication by Prof. Douglas in my *Orientalia Antiqua*, part I. of *The Calendar of the Hia dynasty*, which bear astronomical evidences of its genuineness 2000 B.C., points to a settlement more southern than afterwards under the Chöu dynasty. The Chinese culture spread very early and extensively in the south, and more on the western than on the eastern side. The phonetic writing, propagated by the Chinese immigrants, was eagerly adopted by the active and intelligent population of the South-West. We see them at different periods of Chinese history carrying books to the Chinese court. In 1109 B.C. the Annamites had a phonetic writing, and in several instances we have tidings bearing on the existence of such writings, composed of a certain number of Chinese simple characters used according to the phonetic principle disused amongst the Chinese, as we largely know. These simple characters, selected by progressive elimination of the less easy to draw and to combine, formed a special script, of which we know several offshoots, and have been, according to my views, and as far as affinities of shape and tradition are to be trusted, the *Grundschrift* with which has been framed that splendid monument of Brahmanic phonetic lore—the South Indian Alphabet or Lat-Pali. The North Indian Alphabet has been framed on a Semitic ground according to the same principles, and this achievement has been most likely done at the same time for the two alphabets, as they bear obvious marks of reciprocal influence and of internal making up. Their artificial assimilation and parallelism is obvious. The vocalic notation, however, seems to me to have originated from the South Alphabet side, as here only are found independent vowel characters, which embodied in the consonants have most likely suggested the external addition of marks for the vocalic notation; these marks were reversed to the left for adaptation to the Northern alphabet. Mention has been lately made of a new writing found at Babylon, which by a too hasty conclusion has been on insufficient examination considered as the ancestor of the South Indian Alphabet. But a keen study of those two lines of writing, on a contract clay-tablet of Babylon, dated in the 23rd year of Artaxerxes, has given me a quite different result; they are the signatures in cursive Aramaic of the witnesses of the contract, excepting two who were not acquainted with writing. The interesting feature is, besides its cursive shape, that of the appended consonants, as was occasionally done in cursive Cuneiform; I cannot find any vocalic notation.

rendering of the meaning, the substitution of ideographical characters to others which were less so, became a necessity to them, in order that the meaning might speak to the eye of the reader. But, at the same time, by an association of the respect due to the old texts, in accordance with the great veneration always felt by the Chinese for anything handed down from their ancestors, they thought themselves bound in each possible case to substitute a character homophonous to the sound they could, by tradition, or otherwise, attribute to the old and unsatisfactory one.

27. As to the *Yh-King*, there was happily in these transcriptions from one style into another, a serious barrier, opposed to too numerous changes, in the great veneration in which the written words of the sages of yore were held, quite special in the case of this mysterious classic, with consequently a certain kind of fear of altering them. Otherwise we may be sure that the substitution of characters, if carried to the same extent as has been done in the case of the Shu-King,[1] where it seems that the alterations reached to a full quarter of the total number of the characters, would have been much more considerable.

But as the addition of ideographic determinatives to old characters or groups, could be done without, in their views, altering the sound or the appearance, the process was much more largely followed than any other.[2] As to the mean-

---

[1] In comparing the remains of the Ku-wen text of the Classics engraved on Stone (published in the 三字石經) with the modern text, we find that no less than *twenty-five* per cent. of the characters have been substituted or altered through the transcriptions.

[2] The praise and censure system, which is so conspicuously applied by the commentators of the texts of Confucius, seems to have been really put forward by the Great Sage himself. We know that Confucius said, speaking of the *Ch'un Ts'iu:* "Its righteous decisions I ventured to make." And also: "Yes! It is the *Ch'un Ts'iu* which will make men know me; and it is the *Ch'un Ts'iu* which will make men condemn me" (Vid. Legge, *Chin. Class.*, vol. v. prol. 2). This important statement has been repeated by Mencius and enlarged by him. There is no doubt about its genuineness. Turning to the pages of the *Ch'un Ts'iu*, "We experienced, says Dr. Legge (*ibid*), an intense feeling of disappointment. Instead of a history of events woven artistically together, we find a congeries of the briefest possible intimations of matters in which the Court and State of Lu were more or less concerned, extending over 242 years, without the slightest tincture of literary ability in the composition, or the slightest indication of judicial opinion on the part of the writer." It is a bare ephemeris. This is a difficulty which has still to be solved. The attempt by the commentators, of finding in almost

ings of the characters in the case of the addition of ideographical determinatives, two cases have arisen. The transcribers may or may not have added the proper determinative to determine the exact meaning with which the old character was used in the particular case. In difficult instances the context was of great help, as in the Shu-King, or in the wings of the *Yh*, where special phrases are found. But when the sense of the context is of no help, or does not exist, the problem could by them only be solved by an arbitrary or guessed interpretation, which they expressed, however, in their transcription, by the same system of adding ideographical determinatives.

It is necessary for us to remember these facts, as they show how unavoidably large has been the influence of the ideas and prejudiced views of the epochs on the works of the transcribers.[1]

every paragraph some righteous decision, has laid them open to many absurdities (Legge, *ibid*, p. 5). Now if we consider that according to the principles of writing at the time of the Sage, a greater importance was given, since She Chöu, to the ideographic values of the characters, and that the writer, in order to suggest a complementary idea or fix its meaning, could add an ideographic aphone, we are not far from the explanation. And then if we examine the text, we are sure that here is the solution. So, for instance, whilst recording the deaths of great officers, princes, rulers of states, etc., he made use of 卒 = 'finish,' when he has to record the deaths of the sovereigns of his state (Lu), or of their wives, he used the character 薨 = 'obscure' (to which has been substituted in Siao-chuen style 薨) to show the respect to which those dead were entitled ; it did not allow to consider them as 'finished,' as it was more proper to say that they became obscure and could no more be seen. Again in the records of murders, when the murderer is of the same rank or superior to the killed, Confucius used the ordinary character 殺 = 'to kill'; but when it is the murder of a ruler by a subject or of a father by a son, the Sage uses another character 弑, which he framed himself for the purpose: he substituted for the determinative 殳 'to kill,' the character 式 'rule,' 'pattern,' to show his censure of the fact. I shall study this more largely elsewhere. There is, about the transcriptions made from the old Kuwen texts into the Si-shu, Siao-chuen, and finally the modern style, a curious remark to make. It is the great influence of this system of praise and censure on the selection of substituted characters, the addition of ideographic determinatives, in fact all the modifications introduced by the transcribers. It produces the same effect as if they had endeavoured to transform every text into a smooth stream of righteous principles and moral conduct. Almost in every case where we can restore the old texts, we find in them much more energy and precision.

[1] These various influences of ideographism, and of interpretations by the transcribers, have also to be taken into account in any complete study of old Chinese grammar. The European scholars who have worked upon the ideology, phonetism, and morphology of the Chinese language in the classics, have not yet been able to appreciate the difference which the ideographic transcription they have in hand has produced upon the old style they have not. They were not

IV. OBVIOUS VESTIGES OF THE OLD TEXT.

28. On the old text of the *Yh-King* very little direct information is at hand, and I shall have to find some that is indirect. As it is certainly embodied in the present text, my task in my translation will be to find it out through a minute study of this text, checked by the history of the language and writing in which it is written.

Of the Kwas I shall not say much, as they are not my immediate purpose. Their original delineation is connected, as we have seen, with the writing of the tortoise. Traditions repeatedly found in literature mention the map of the Ho river and the writing of the Lo river. The great appendix of the Yh says: "The Ho 河 gave forth the map and the Lo 洛 gave forth the writing, which the sages took as pattern."[1] It is further said in the Li-Ki[2] that "the map was borne by a horse 馬 " and elsewhere that the writing was on the back of a divine tortoise.[3] This statement has been repeated by Confucius, and it requires an explanation. Throwing off the legendary apparatus of style with which they are traditionally reported, we find in these events two very simple facts. The Tortoise writing given forth by the Loh river is very likely the finding of a large tortoise shell of which the lineaments answered to a certain disposition of numbers.[4] As to the map produced by the Ma 馬 from the Ho river, we have to suggest that it was nothing else than one of these numerical inscriptions, afterwards improved

---

aware how highly artificial is the written language, and how deep is the abyss which separates it from the colloquial, modern and ancient, which, after all, is the only one interesting for linguistic research. The phonetic decipherment of the old Ku-wen texts when available will enable Sinologists to know something of the old spoken language. The readings, we have found out, make it clear that the use of frequent polysyllabics or compounds did not, in the old time any more than in the present, let so much looseness in the grammatical value and meaning of the words that was supposed to have existed. Besides that, the phonetism more full of the separate words (not decayed as now) did not present in the old spoken language so many homophones leading to confusion, as was dremised by the ancient Sinologists.

[1] *Vid. Hi-se*, part i. sect. 79.
[2] *Vid. Li-ki*, ch. viii. trad. Callery, p. 50, Turin, 1853, 4to.
[3] *Vid. Lun-yü*, ix. 8.
[4] Among the 1690 works quoted by the Imperial compilers of the *Tai-Ping-yü-Lan* in 977-983 are twelve works on the *Ho-tu*, two on the *Loh-shu*, and one on them both.

into an arithmetical puzzle, of cup marks as found in India on cliffs and rocks or banks of rivers, and connected somehow with a native tribe of which the name has been frequently expressed phonetically by a character meaning a horse.[1]

At any rate, the two objects, whatever they were, are enumerated in the Shu-King among the treasures kept at the Chinese court as late as 1079 B.C., where we find mentioned, the *Ho tu* 河 圖, the great Tortoise-shell, etc.[2]

29. If the Kwas, which were a survival of the arrows of divination known to the ancestors of Chinese culture before their emigration eastward,[3] have been traced out from the lineaments of the tortoise shell, we should suppose that the plain lines and the broken lines were intended to represent the non-crossed and the crossed lineaments; and if from the thrown divining rods also, from the same fact of their relative positions of crossed or non-crossed over. But now we arrive at speculations void and fruitless, and it is time to stop.

30. In the Shu-King we find an extensive allusion to divination, as done by the Duke of Chöu, who consulted the oracular lines kept in the Royal Treasury, and we know from the *Chöu Li* that "the forms of the regular prognostications were in all 120, the explanations of which amounted to 1200."[4] Are we to take these numbers literally? Could not we suppose that we have here an indication of the two rows of each hexagram, which seems to have been the main division of the Kwei-Tsang, and in six times this number their division according to the lines; this hypothesis would prove satisfactory if we had 128 and 1248, instead of 120 and 1200, given perhaps as round numbers. Or, have we here quite a different system of oracular lines? This might be, as

---

[1] The extraordinary similarity between the Ho map and the inscriptions found in India by Mr. H. Rivett Carnac is too striking to be neglected. See his *Rough Notes on some Ancient Sculpturings on Rocks in Kamaon*, in *Journal of the Royal Asiatic Society of Bengal*, 1877, vol. xlvi. pp. 1-15. I have already pointed out this similarity in my paper on *The Indo-Chinese Origin of the South Indian Writing*.

[2] Vid. *Shu-King*, part v. bk. 22. The great precious tortoise is also mentioned as an heirloom in *The Great Announcement*, about 1115 B.C. See Chinese Classics, ed. Legge, iii. p. 365.

[3] Cf. my *Early History of the Chinese Civilisation*, p. 30.

[4] See Legge, *Chinese Classics*, vol. iii. p. 356 n.

the Duke of Chöu consulted the tortoise[1] instead of the milfoil usually employed for the divination by the diagram.[2]

31. We have seen above that the two Yhs, earlier than Chöu's Yh, were the *Lien-Shan* under the Hia dynasty (2205-1766) and the *Kwei-Tsang* under the Yn dynasty (1766-1122 B.C.), both including the sixty-four Kwas.[3]

The *Lien-Shan* does not seem to have had the text divided between the sixty-four Kwas, but only under eight divisions or perhaps the eight principal Kwas, as the tradition says that its text was composed of eight myriads of words.[4] This agrees to a certain extent with the meaning of the name *Lien-Shan* = "united mountains," by which we can understand

---

[1] In the *Tso-Chuen* we find several references to this different system, of which it may be interesting to quote one here: in 635 B.C. *The Marquis Wen* made the master of divination, Yen, consult the tortoise shell about the undertaking. *He did so* and said, "The oracle is auspicious,—that of Hwang-ti's battle in Fan-ts'iun." The marquis said, "that oracle is too great for me." The diviner replied, "The rules of Chöu are not changed. The King of to-day is the Emperor of Antiquity." The marquis *then* said, "Try it by the milfoil." They consulted the reeds and found the diagram, etc., etc. See Legge, *Chinese Classics*, vol. v. p. 195.

[2] In the same work, fourth part of *The Great Plan*, we read an interesting instruction^a about the divination to be practised in case of doubts:

"Seventhly, on the examination of doubts 七 稽 疑. Select and appoint *special* officers to divine 擇 建 立 卜 筮 人. And as to the orders to divine,^b 乃 命 卜 筮, *they are* called *rain* 曰 雨, called *clearing up* 曰 霽, called *cloudiness* 曰 蒙, called *disconnected* 曰 驛, called *crossing* 曰 克, called *correctness* 曰 貞, called *repentance* 曰 悔. Of these seven 凡 七 divine by the tortoise five 卜 五, and as prognostics use *the other* two 占 用 二, to trace out the errors 衍 忒.

As we have most probably here a relic of the Hia dynasty, it is interesting to find in it this statement of seven orders, or perhaps sets of slips for divination. I shall examine elsewhere what connexion, if any, may have existed between these seven orders and the meanings attributed to the eight diagrams, two of which agree. It would seem that we have here seven series indicated or divining slips instead of eight, which, one may suppose, was the number of classes of rows of characters used in the consultation for prognostics in the *Lien Shan* system.

NOTES.—^a I find a rather different translation in 85 words in Dr. Legge's *Chinese Classics*, vol. iii. p. 335, but with the addition of so many words which are not in the text, that I prefer to give a more literal translation.—^b 命 translated 'decree of divination.' Cf. Medhurst's *Shoo-King*, The Great Announcement, p. 217.

[3] In fact the period 1766-1122 includes two dynasties, the *Shang* from 1766 to 1401, and the *Yn* afterwards; but this last name is also given to the whole period.

[4] Vid. *Tai-Ping Yü lan*, K. 608, f. 5. 入 萬 as usual is not to be taken literally 80,000, but as meaning eight indeterminate innumerable quantities.

the lack of the distinctions and distributions afterwards introduced.

The *Kwei-tsang*="returned treasures," by which meaning we understand the attributions of the meanings to the Kwas and their parts,[1] is a little more known to us, though the very text *eo nomine* no longer exists as an independent and separate work. We have seen that it had a certain division of the text in two parts, probably according to the inner and outer diagram of each hexagram, and it seems likely that these two parts in every chapter were again divided in six. The text was composed of four thousand three hundred words.[2]

32. The documentary evidences on the old text of the *Yh* are of several kinds. Some consist of the quotations in other classics, others are the result of internal indications, and also the palæographical proofs.

We have already (§ 18) spoken of an evidence of prime importance in the score of quotations given in the *Tso-Chuen*. They do not always agree with the text as we have it, and the discrepancies are not in every case those which can be attributed to clerical transcriptions. The discrepancies exhibited by the quotations indicated where they divine by the milfoil and before they indicate the Yh of Chöu, point certainly to an old text which has been wilfully modified in the *Yh* of Chöu. In elucidating my version I hope to show all these discrepancies, and in several cases

---

[1] It is not unlikely that something of the arrangement by Wen Wang has crept out from the temporary homonymy at his time of these two characters, *Kwei-tsang* with 歸 and 貞. Cf. above, § 2 n. This will be discussed in the translation.

[2] Though the text of the *Kwei-Tsang* 歸藏 seems to have been lost of old, quotations from it were found in old literature. The work is not one of the 1690 works of which the titles are given at the beginning of the Great Cyclopædia of 983 A.D., the *Tai Ping Yü lan*. However several quotations from it are given in it, and I think it interesting to reproduce them. In the chapter on *Nü Kwa*

女媧, we read: 歸藏曰昔女媧筮張雲慕枚占之曰吉昭昭九州日月代極平均土地和合四國.

In the chapter on *Hwang-Ti* we read: 歸藏曰昔黃神與炎神爭鬭涿鹿之野將戰筮於巫咸曰果哉而有咎.

Vid. K. 78, f. 4, and K. 79, f. 2. On *Nü Kwa*, vid. Mayer's Manual, p. 162, n. 521.

the causes of their modification, by Wen Wang; but we have no room here for such an investigation.

33. It would be also beyond the scope of these pages to show the serious differences of style between that of the Text, in the case of phrases, and that of the oldest wings, the *Twan* and the *Siang*, works of Wen Wang and of Chöu Kung. They are not all of the same period, the Text exhibiting an older stage of grammar. Many peculiarities of style in the Text are not of those which have been introduced by the western influence of the Chöu, and consequently, as they cannot be more modern, they point to an older period. It is a fact of the evolution of the language, which I have traced up and explained elsewhere, but my present version points out the many materials which the text of the *Yh* offers for that purpose.

34. Another argument, the several cases of which I am able to point out in my version, is in connection with the foretelling words, showing their ulterior addition to the primitive text in accord with what we know by the tradition as has been shown above (§ 13). It is that in the rhymed chapters, they are outside the rhymes! The importance of this fact must not be neglected, as it shows that the text was written before its partition into separate lines to correspond to the weak and strong lines of the Kwas, and before the intermingling of the words of fate.

35. A careful study of the *Ku-wen* text of the *Yh* would be of the greatest importance. It would certainly discriminate the alterations introduced by Wen Wang: I, therefore, await anxiously the good chance which may put in my hands, or in those of any one of more ability, the text *Ku-wen* handed down by *Fei-shi*, a text which was not different from the Imperial copy revised by Liu Hiang about the Christian era, at the time of the Literary Revival under the Han dynasty, as will be seen below (§ 48).

The numerous palæographical works compiled with great care by the Chinese (several of which would do honour to European scholars), and the comparison with many inscriptions, afford a not inconsiderable amount of information towards the recognition of the old meanings of the characters, besides their values in the Shu-King and the Shi-King. But all this requires a good deal of patient research and comparative criticism for a profitable use of them.

36. In the absence of the continuous text of the *Yh* in old *Ku-wen* characters, we are not altogether deprived of certain tidings, and though they cannot, as the text would do, give us the same amount of information, they are not to be neglected. There are two means for finding them, first, by the palæography, and secondly by the traditions in literature.

Characters of the *Ku-wen* text of the *Yh* are found in Chinese palæographical works,[1] and some have occasionally been quoted by the late M. Pauthier from the text of *Fei-shi* which he possessed in his own library. Though these characters are not numerous, they are not without their utility for our researches. The comparative studies I have made for my history of the Chinese language, on the transformations of the Chinese characters from the most ancient period downwards, allow me to say what we learn from these characters quoted from the old *Yh-King*. They concur in fully strengthening the exactitude of the traditions quoted above on the existence of the old text of the *Yh*, or the greatest part of it, long before the time of Wen Wang, its partial modification, completion and arrangement by that sage, and the authorship of the *Twan* and *Siang* by the same and by his son.

37. These characters are of three kinds. Some, which come from the text, are of the oldest period when the writing was the faithful reproduction of the language. This stage had passed away at the time of Wen Wang and his

---

[1] Such as the 六書分類 by Fu Lwan Tsiang, 1751, in 14 Kiuen, according to the 214 radicals; the 六書通 by 閔齊伋, 1661, in 10 Kiuen, according to 76 finals. In these two works the old forms are quoted with references to the inscriptions, texts, etc., where they are to be found. The latter, though less complete than the former, is more accurate; it is a wonderful monument of palæographical knowledge and patient research, the work of an entire life devoted to study. Its author published it at the age of 82. It has been reprinted several times, in 1718, 1796, 1865, and these are the different editions I have seen; the 1796 one is the worst.

son. Other characters, from the *Twan* and *Siang*, and occasionally from the text, are also of the old style still in use, with or without additional ideographic determinatives, but no longer understood on the principles of their composition and hence blindly copied. The third category includes characters from the wings, which are obviously written according to the principles laid down by *She Chöu* about 820 B.C. We shall not enter into the details, they would be most interesting, about these categories, as they would require more space than we can afford. We cannot help, however, quoting two or three examples of the oldest written words.

38. So 恆 *heng*, constant, continual, which in the Ku wen text of the *Yh* was written by a group of two characters which transcribed in modern caligraphy would be 亙 丂 Reading the two characters according to the orthographical principles of the old Ku-wen, we expect, by their disposition side by side, a compound word to be read from left to right, and we find 亙 *Keng* 丂 *Kiao*, which is obviously the same as the modern expression *heng kiu* 恆 久, having the same meaning.[2] In the *Twan* and *Siang* we find two forms of the same early group, but of which the component parts were no longer understood, as shown by the blind interpretation given to their strokes.[3]

Again, 頤 *I* 'the chin,' which represents two characters of the older *Yh*, 臣 and 頤; one is the heading of the 27th chapter, the other is in the text.[4] We shall see in our version which spoken expression it represents.

Again 解 substitution in modern writing to the *Siao Chuen*

---

[1] Cf. Min tsi Ki, *Luh shu t'ung*, K. iv. f. 21 v. Fu Lwan Tsiang, *Luh shu Fön Luy*, s.v.

[2] In cases of single words written phonetically with two characters, these are often superposed; the under one suggesting the initial. These principles and their ulterior modifications, their demonstration and the method which I have used to find them, are explained and summarized in my paper on the Evolution of Language and Writing in China. Vid. also the notes to § 23 of the present paper.

[3] Min Tsi Ki, *Luh shu t'ung*, K. i. f. 29.

[4] This is one of the characters which show that the writing borrowed by the Bak people, *Pöh Sing*, has not always been written in perpendicular lines. As all those which had more width than height, it has been turned up from the right, and originally represented the lower part of the face, mouth, and chin, still discernible through the modern strokes.

荔 which had been substituted for the *Ku-wen* 卽.[1] Read according to the old principles, the latter gives mod. *Kih tsieh*, and in the oldest dialects *K'ich tiet* (Sinico-Annamite), or *Kwik tsit* (Canton), which are no longer used, but for which we find the modern equivalent 解說 *Kiai shet*, Pekinese *Chieh-shuo*, to explain, to unloose.

If space could be given to this question, many proofs could be forthcoming to show that Wen Wang has entirely misunderstood the materials he had in hand. For example, he has misunderstood an old group form of 姤 'a girl' (44th Kwa) for 姤 *copulatio*; but, as this subject would have been unfit for discussion, he has been unable to follow this course in his arrangement of the text, so that the whole chapter, which describes the occupations of a girl, presents now in the modern interpretation an amount of nonsense, seldom found to so ludicrous an extent.

39. Tradition has been kept of the modifications (transcribed in modern character), introduced by Wen Wang to twenty-five of the sixty-four headings of the chapters.[2] He has put at the Kwa 5. 需 instead of 濡; 9. 小畜 instead of 毒畜; 15. 謙 instead of 鎌; 18. 蠱 instead of 蜀; 23. 剝 instead of 僕; 25. 天妄 instead of 毋亡; 26. 大畜 instead of 奉畜; 29. 坎 instead of 莘; 31. 咸 instead of 誠; 33. 遯 instead of 遂; 37. 家人 instead of 晢家人; 40. 解 instead of 荔; 41. 損 instead of 員; 46. 升 instead of 稱; 51. 震 instead of 益; 52. 艮 instead of 狠; 59. 渙 instead of 奐.

Besides these seventeen, there are five single headings, 冇, 𧮫, 欽, 規, 夜, and three double 兮䨖, 林䄄, 馬徒, of which Wen Wang's substitutes have not been traditionally kept, but which can be detected without great difficulty, by a close study of the book.

As these headings are the objects of the chapters, it is easy to conceive how important it is to know them with precision,

---

[1] Cf. § 23 n. and Min Tsi Ki, *Luh shu tung*, K. v. f. 33.
[2] Vid. 路史, 餘論, K. 2, f. 2 v.

for the understanding of the rows of characters by which they are followed.

40. Remains of the early commentators [1] show unmistakably a period intermediary between the characters as they have been transcribed into the actual style of writing and the oldest one, fully justifying what we have said of the gradual modification of the characters, according to the views of the interpreters at the successive transcriptions from the old *Ku-wen* text into the *Siao Chuen* style, and from this into the modern *Kiai Shu*.

In the ordinary edition we find that thirty-one headings are the object of special remarks; thirteen are indicated as sham representatives and eighteen are to be taken with a special meaning.

It is in this passage and transcription from the *Siao-Chuen* to the modern style, that in the absence of the *Ku-wen* text, we shall be able in numerous cases to check the interpretation supported by the modern characters. Substitution of characters, as 杞 for 鐋, and 無 for 无, or 濟 for 泲 are not unimportant, but such as 惕 'respectful' for 賜 'pelvis' modifies entirely the possible meaning. And is not the same thing to be said of 豐, 漸, 袘, 絮, 罡, substituted to 豐, 墊, 茒, 袈, 旧, etc., etc.[2]

41. We find in the dictionary of the "Original characters of the thirteen kings," *Shih san King Pön tze* 十三逕本字 sect. of *Yh King*, some changes of characters, as these: 榦 instead of 榦; 確 instead of 确; 簪 instead of 无; 頤 instead of 臣; 肺 instead of 图; 樽 instead of 尊.[3]

Or characters as these: 礬, 遒, 泚, 晢, 衷, 閟, 趾, 腊, 隊, which are but the sham representatives of the older ones.

According to the notes of the ordinary editions of the *Yh*, we find no less than 77 in the text and 102 in the Twan,

---

[1] Cf. the 周易, annotated by 黃頴 of the Tsin period. Vid. 南海縣志, K. 25.

[2] Vid. *Luh-shu-fön-luy*, svv.

[3] So 衷 is for 抰. Cf. Min tsi Ki, *Luh shu t'ung*, K. iv., f. 51.

Siang and Wen Yen embodied with the text, of characters which stand for others, and over 300 which are translated with unusual meanings. Many of the latter show only how forced were the interpretations supposed by the editors. It is instructive to point out these facts as a warning for those who should be inclined to accept any version, which has not been prepared by the necessary palæographical and linguistic researches on the text; a scientific preparation of which the Chinese interpreters in their attempts, and the European as well, though less excusable, do not seem to have had the slightest idea.

V.—The Native Interpretations.

42. The possibility of understanding certain parts of the *Yh-King*, such as the ethnological chapters and the legendary ballads, led early to the conclusion, that the whole of these documents could be currently read and interpreted. It is quite possible that the hexagrams[1] were attached to them merely as a system of numerical classification to keep them in proper order; but it is more likely that the antiquity of these obscure documents, and the tradition that they contained a treasure of ancient wisdom, first led to their use as fateful and prophetic sentences, in which some glimmer of meaning was detected or surmised, and that the hexagrams were then applied to them for the purposes of divination.

The attempt to explain these old fragments began early, and has been continued by a host of scholars. The selection of 1450 works on the *Yh* for the library of Kien-Lung points to anything but unanimity in the understanding of the book.

43. The profound modifications which were introduced by Wen Wang, in his transcription of the old text, are attested by the precise and exact traditions respecting his work, which we have quoted above (§§ 12, 13, 14, 38, 39). But

---

[1] On the possible connexion of the Kwas with the belomancy of S.W. Asia, the eight Kwas of Fuh-hi and the eight arrows of Marduk, see my *Early history of Chinese civilization*, p. 29-30.

the method he pursued in his treatment of the text, and more markedly still in the explanations (*Twan*) he appended to each chapter, is made clearer to us by the work of later commentators. The book itself, as it stands now, bears obvious traces of many discrepancies of views, as we shall see hereafter.

Wen Wang meditated upon the old sets of words appended to each leading character, title or subject of each chapter, and modified some of these characters to suit his fanciful interpretation of the context or sequel. He worked hard to make something of them and to accommodate them at all risks to some sort of signification. He expanded them so as to fill up the seven lines he wanted for each chapter, and he is open to the suspicion of having added more than the prognosticating words, when his materials were not sufficient. When the primitive text at his disposal was too short for his purpose, the same meanings are severally repeated; but when the contrary happens, the meanings are piled up one after the other, with an attempt to make out some kind of sense, which is necessarily broken and disconnected; except in a few cases where, either by chance or by ability in modifying the characters by their homonyms or synonyms, some kind of connected meaning has been obtained. It should be observed, with reference to those chapters which are mere lists of meanings, that the very nature of the case made it an easier task to force a general internal connexion upon them, because of the occasional relation of the meanings, primitive or derived.

44. Wen Wang has arranged the *Yh* documents, exchanging characters, sometimes for their homonyms, sometimes for their synonyms; he has displaced some in order to give the prominence to characters which could be taken as foretelling words; and of such words he has interpolated not a few. He has ingeniously tried to give to the whole of every chapter an appearance of relation to the special symbolic meanings attributed to each of the two trigrams composing the hexagram, and, in so doing, has led the way for subsequent commentators, among whom his son Tan holds a prominent

place. He has written the *Twan*, which may be taken as a justification of the text as amended by him, and which gives hints on the symbolism he thought was embodied in the hexagrams.

45. If Wen Wang had actually evolved from his brain all these incongruous and more or less disconnected words, we might conclude that his confinement in Yu-li had seriously affected his mental power, since, if we take all the chapters for a genuine text, it is just such a composition as might have emanated from a lunatic asylum. The only possibility of avoiding such a conclusion is to admit, what is shown by various kinds of evidence, that he could not help using sets of characters and meanings framed a long time beforehand for each chapter, and that he did his best with them.[1]

46. The *Yh-King*, with the Five commentaries, as arranged by Confucius, was handed down by one of the disciples of the Sage, called *Shang Kiu*[2] 商 瞿, and styled *Tze Muh* 子 木, of whom we know very little. Was it he who embodied into two of the wings the quotations of Confucius' words, or was it *Puh Shang* 卜 商, styled *Tze Hia* 子 夏, another of the disciples of the Sage, who is said to have written on the *Yh* a commentary in eleven books?[3] The *Records of the Former Han Dynasty*[4] report that the *Yh* was commented on during the Civil war period by numerous schools, but in fact we have only the names of those of the Han period. The next most important commentary seems[5] to have been

---

[1] Chu Chen 朱 震 has remarked (*Han Kien Lui Han*, K. 195, f. 15v.), that Wen Wang made the *Yh* in such a manner that the Kwas 乾 坤 坎 離 compose the first, and that 艮 兌 震 巽 compose the second book. These Kwas, which are the eight primitive ones, are classified in the present arrangement as Nos. 1, 2, 29, and 30, in the first book, and 52, 58, 51, and 57, in the second. Should any additional proofs be necessary to show that the increase of 8 to 64 was made previously to Wen Wang, this anomaly of arrangement would be one.
[2] On Shang Kiu, see *Tsien Han Shu*, K. 88.
[3] *Puh Shang*, born 507 B.C., was yet living in 406 B.C., and then presented copies of some of the Classical Books to the prince Wen of Wei. He is represented as a scholar extensively read and exact, but without great comprehension of mind. See Legge, *Chin. Class.* vol. i. proleg. p. 118, on *Puh Shang*.
[4] See the chapters on Literature, K. 30, f. 1.
[5] See the 易 經 正 義.

that of *T'ien Ho* 田和,¹ the great officer 大夫 who, in 379 B.C., founded the second dynasty of rulers of the state of Ts'i.

Many other scholars and commentators are known to have worked on the *Yh* during the centuries preceding and following the foundation of the Chinese Empire; the names of many and the works of a few are not yet altogether forgotten. They are reputed, by the later interpreters who maintain their own explanations, to have been uniformly in error.

47. When during the Ts'in dynasty the books were burnt (B.C. 213-212), the *Yh* being a book employed for divination was preserved. This is expressly stated by Pan K'u in his *Records of the (Former) Han dynasty* (section of Literature), where he reproduces the famous catalogue compiled in the last years preceding the Christian era, by Liu Hiang, Liu Hin and others, of all the books gathered for the Imperial Library. We reproduce from this catalogue the list concerning the *Yh-King*, as follows:

Yh-King; 12 sections (from) *She* 施, *Möng* 孟, *Liang Kiu* 梁丘 3 schools. (Se Ku says: The upper and lower parts of the classic and the ten wings, namely 12 sections in all.²)

Yh's tradition 傳 (from) *Chöu She* 周氏; 2 sections. (Grandson of *Fu Wang* 孚王孫.³)

—————— *Fuh She* 服氏, 2 sections. (A native of *Tsi* 齊 called *Fuh Kwang* 服光.)

—————— *Yang She* 楊氏, 2 sections. (Named *Ho*, styled *Shu-yuen* 何字叔元, native of *Che-chwen* 菑川 Shan-tung.⁴)

---

¹ See on *Tien Ho*, Mayer's *C.R.M.*, part i. n. 719.
² This is the Imperial copy, revised as said above by Liu-Hiang.
³ Pauthier, *loc. cit.*, who quotes three of these works, says of this second: "Le Yh-King avec les explications de Wen Wang et de Tchéou Koung en deux livres, tel qu'il subsiste encore de nos jours." There are several mistakes in these statements. The Chinese text says nothing of the kind, and Chöu She, in whose name he finds a reference to Wen Wang and Chöu Kung, was a literate of the Han period.
⁴ Probably so called from *Hien-Yang*, the capital of the Ts'in, the archives of which were saved by Siao Ho, who died B.C. 193, whose full name is given in the note. See on him, Mayer's *Chinese Reader's Manual*, n. 578, 601, and *Chinese Classics*, edit. Legge, vol. i. Proleg. p. 118.

THE YH-KING AND ITS AUTHORS. 39

———— *Ts'ai Kung* 蔡公, 2 sections. (Native of Wei 衞, grandson of *She Chöu Wang* 事周王.)
———— *Han She* 韓氏, 2 sections. (Named *Ing* 嬰.[1])
———— *Wang She* 王氏, 2 sections. (Named *Tung* 同.)
———— *Ting She* 丁氏, 2 sections. (Named *Kw'an*, styled *Tze*, 寬字子, native of Siang Liang.)
———— *Ku Wu Tze* 古五子, 18 sections. (From 甲子 to 壬子 taught the Yn and Yang of the *Yh* 說易陰陽.[2])
———— *Hwei Nan's*[3] Right-path Precepts 淮南道訓, 2 sections. (*Hwai Nan Wang* facilitated the researches and explanations of the *Yh*, and nine men studied the rules of the nine masters.)
———— Old Miscellanies 古雜, 80 sections.
———— Discriminations of Miscellaneous calamities 雜災異, 35 sections.
———— 'Spiritual gyration' 神輸, 5 sections and one Map.
———— *Möng She* and *King Fang*[4] 孟氏京房, 11 sections.
———— id.   id.   66 sections.
———— *Luh ch'ung tsung lioh shwoh* 鹿克宗略說, 3 sections.
———— *King she ha kia* 京氏叚嘉, 12 sections.
———— Various extracts (from) *She, Möng* and *Liang Kin* 章句施孟梁丘, each 2 sections.

Altogether 13 schools and 294 sections.

In the chapter *on divination* of the "Catalogue" of Liu

---

[1] Probably Töu Yng, who died B.C. 131. See on this officer, Mayer's *Manual*, part i. n. 678.
[2] From 57 to 9 B.C. As there is no other indication, we must take the cyclical characters as indicating the nearest period from the author's compilation—perhaps that *Ku Wu Tze* is to be translated *The Old Five Masters*. The statement is very important for the history of the Yh commentaries, even when a different view is maintained, as in 淵鑑類函, K. 192, f. 19.
[3] Or *Liu Ngan*, who died B.C. 122. See Mayer's *Manual*, part i. n. 412.
[4] On King Fang, philosopher and astronomer, of the first century B.C., see Mayer's *C.R.M.* part i. n. 270. In the list of 1690 works given as references by the compilers of the Cyclopedia *Tai-Ping Yü Lan*, eight works connected with the *Yh* and divination are by or on King Fang.

Hiang and Liu Yn, there are several titles of books on the Changes, as follows:—

周 易, 38 Kiuen.—周 易 明 室, 26 K.—周 易 隨 曲 射 匡, 50 K.—大 筮 衍 易, 28 K.—大 次 雜 易, 30 K.—於 陵 欽 易 吉 凶, 23 K.—任 眞 易 旗, 71 K.—易 卦 入 具.

48. At the time that the Han dynasty rose to power, the explanations of *Tien Ho* 田 和 were still followed. Down to the dates of the Emperors *Süan* 宣 (73–48 B.C.) and *Yuen* 元 (48–32 B.C.), the *Yh* was commented on by *She Ch'öu* 施 讎, *Möng Hi* 孟 喜, *Liang Kiu* 梁 丘 in the official literary schools, and by *Fei chi* 費 直, *King Fang* 京 房 and *Kao* 高.[1] Among the people *Liu-Hiang* took the Imperial *Ku-wen* 古 文 text of the *Yh-King*, and collated it with the editions of *She*, *Möng* and *Liang Kiu*; occasionally he omitted passages which did not exist (in the olden text), or which were faulty, and restored others which had been lost. But *Fei's* edition[2] was identical with the *Ku-wen*,[3] and this scholar had studied the *Yh* of *T'ien Ho*, which with the commentaries formed twelve *pien*. So had done *She*, *Möng*, *Liang* and *Tsü Tung*, but without following the very words of *T'ien Ho's* commentary.[4]

49. *Yang Hiung* (B.C. 53–A.D. 18), the author of the famous *Vocabulary of Dialects* 方 言, wrote the *T'ai hüen King* 太 玄 經,[5] professedly in elucidation of the *Yh-King*,

---

[1] The text of Pan Ku gives only the names as She, Möng, and Liang Kiu, but we complete them from the 周 易 正 義 in *Tai-Ping-yü-lan*, K. 609, f. 2.

[2] The late French sinologist, G. Pauthier, possessed in his own library an edition of the Ku-wen text of the Yh, printed in 1596, under the title 周易全書古文 in 2 *pien*. His valuable library having been broken up and dispersed everywhere, I have been unable to find this book. We have to regret that Pauthier could not follow his scheme of publishing it in facsimile. And so, too, we have to regret that he has not given somewhere a description of it. He only says that it was the text of Fei-chi (probably 費 直). Should this edition be genuine, it would be of immense importance for our studies. Vid. Pauthier, *Journal Asiatique*, Sept.–Oct. 1867, p. 238, and Avril-Mai, 1868, p. 363.

[3] Pauthier (*Journal Asiatique*, Sept.–Oct., 1867, pp. 236–238) has misunderstood all these passages. He has mistaken: 1°. the names of the two Emperors Süen and Yuen for the name of a commentator who never existed; 2°. The name of Möng, a commentator of the first century B.C., for the name of Mencius; 3°. he has made of Liang-Kiu, also a commentator of the Han period, two men; taking *Liang* as *Koh Liang* and *Kiu* as Confucius.

[4] Vid. 易 說 序.

[5] His book in the *Tai-Ping-yu-lan*, is quoted as 楊 雄 易 太 元 經.

but it is considered almost as obscure as the original classic. His views were upheld by *Se-Ma Kwang* (A.D. 1009-1086), and in recent times by *Tsiao-Yuen-hi*, but, after all, the result is unsatisfactory.[1]

The application of the old theory of the two principles, *Yn* and *Yang*, Obscurity and Light, Female and Male activities in Nature (which has been lately carried through the whole *Yh* by Canon MacClatchie in his English version), had been made to the *Yh-King* during the first century B.C., as we have seen in the catalogue of Lin Hiang.[2]

Another celebrated commentary of the Han period was written by Tsiao Kan 焦 贛.[3]

50. Almost everything has been sought for in the *Yh*, inasmuch as the unintelligibility of the text was an asylum for any freak of imagination. As early as the middle of the second century B.C. the *Yh* was connected with alchemy.[4] The earliest work now extant on the practice of alchemy, according to Mr. A. Wylie, is the *Ts'an t'ung K'i* 參 同 契, from the hand of Wei Peh-yang 魏 伯 陽.[5] This writer professes to discover the occult science hidden in the mysterious symbols of the *Yh-King*, but his book and his doctrine have been by common consent discarded by the literati. Many commentaries have been written on this treatise, the most important being under the Tang, the Sung and the Yuen dynasties.[6]

Kwoh P'oh (A.D. 276-324), a famous scholar, commentator and expositor of the doctrines of the Taoist transcendentalism, also ventured an explanation of the *Yh-King*.[7]

The character 元 is for 玄, because the latter being the personal name of the Emperor K'ang Hi, forbidden during the reign of the Emperor, was still left aside at the time of the reprint of the Cyclopedia.

[1] *Vid.* Wylie, *Notes on Chinese Literature*, p. 69.
[2] Others are enumerated by Dr. J. H. Plath, *Ueber die Sammlung Chinesischer Werke der Staatsbibliothek aus der Zeit der D. Han und Wei*. München, 1868, 8vo. pp. 4, 5.
[3] On this philosopher *vid.* Mayer's *Chinese Reader's Manual*, n. 839.
[4] Many are indicated in Matwanlin, *Wen hien tung K'ao*, K. 175.
[5] In the *Tai-Ping-yü-lan* it is quoted under the title of 周 易 *Ts'an t'ung K'i*, which is the name given by the commentator P'ang Hian of the Tang period.
[6] For more details *Vid.* Wylie, *Notes on Chinese Literature*, p. 175.
[7] *Vid.* 郭 璞 易 洞 林.

51. Down to the time of the Wei dynasty 魏 (220-265 A.D.) the doctrines of *She-Ch'öu* and *Möng-Hi* had schools and were discussed. But at the time of the Western Tsin 西晉 (265-313 A.D.) the schools of *Liang Kiu, She Ch'öu* and *Kao* disappear;[1] those of *Möng-Hi* and *King-Fang* were still known by their books, but they were no longer taught. The teachings of *Fei-chi* were commented upon by *Chang-Hüan* 鄭玄 (A.D. 127-200),[2] under the Eastern Han dynasty, and later on by *Wang-Pi* 王弼 (A.D. 226-249),[3] under the Wei dynasty. The latter was a scholar of high repute, and deeply versed in the mystic lore of the *Yh-King*;[4] notwithstanding the early age (24) at which he died, his erudition was such as to cause him to be looked upon in subsequent ages as the founder of the modern philosophy of divination.

52. The theories of *Wang-Pi* on the subject remained unchallenged until the period of the Sung dynasty, when a fresh school was founded by Chen-Hi-I 陳希夷 or Ch'en-Tw'an 陳摶 (who died about A.D. 920).[5] This celebrated Taoist philosopher and recluse had devoted himself to the study of the arts of alchemy and the occult philosophy of the *Yh-King*. He is recognized by Chu-Hi as having founded the modern school of interpretation of the system of the diagrams.[6] But according to the compilers of the Imperial edition, down to the time of Chu-Hi or Chu-Futze (1130-1200), the essence of the *Yh-King* had not been understood, and to this great philosopher is attributed the honour of having made it known to the great advantage of his compatriots. The *Yh* has been interpreted by Chu-Futze and his fellow authors of the Sung dynasty, as a treatise on morals, a directory for self-government and politics,—a view, however, which had been introduced by Cheng Futze. Though the great influence of Chu-Hi's commentaries

---

[1] *Vid.* 京房易傳, reprinted in the *Han Wei t'sung shu* collection.
[2] *Vid.* on these two celebrated scholars, Mayer's *Chinese Reader's Manual*, nn. 59 and 812.
[3] *Vid.* 周易正義 in *Tai Ping yü lan*, K. 609, f. 2.
[4] His book is entitled 周易略例, reprinted in the *Han Wei t'sung shu* collection.
[5] *Vid.* Mayer's *Chinese Reader's Manual*, p. 245.
[6] *Vid.* Mayer, *ibid.*

on the other classics, and the just recognition of his services to Chinese literature, have given to his views an undeserved repute, and have rather overshadowed the other systems of interpreting the *Yh*, the latter have by no means been silenced.

53. Writers of the present dynasty, such as Hwei-T"ing-ü, Chang-Hwei-yen and others, who have accomplished a positive advance towards freedom of thought in their study of the ancient books, have drawn attention to the old interpretations of authors who lived early in the Christian era. They regard the *Yh* rather as a book of fate. According to them it foreshadows the changes of the physical universe and of human affairs. It is the record of the unseen destiny that controls the prosperity and decay which belong to all beings and things. Its symbols are of so general a kind that they admit of various applications; but the most distinctly marked of these applications are to the accession of an emperor to the throne, and the distinction between the good and noble-minded man and one who possesses the opposite qualities. These more ancient critics lived very near the time of the disciples of Confucius, and are therefore considered to have been in a better position for ascertaining the real meaning of the book than later scholars. Some of them were Taoists, to which religion the happy obscurity of this book accommodates itself as well as to the Confucian.[1]

54. These few sketches (§§ 42–53) are far from conveying to the reader's mind an idea of the multiplicity and variety of the native interpretations of the *Yh-King*. It would be an immense task, far beyond the scope of the present pages, to quote even the bare names of all those who, in China, have laboured on the mysterious book. There is scarcely any of the commentators of the Classics who has not endeavoured to propose new explanations on the whole or in details. Such is their number that in the last century (1772–1790), when the great catalogue for the library of the Emperor Kien-Lung was drawn up, no less than fourteen

---

[1] For part of this section see Dr. Edkins, *On the Present State of Science, Literature, and Literary Criticism in China*, reprinted from the *North China Herald* of March, 1857, in *The Chinese and Japanese Repository*, London, 1864, 8vo. pp. 29, 32, 63-69; cf. p. 67.

hundred and fifty different works on the *Yh* were selected for that purpose. How many more were forgotten, deliberately rejected or lost altogether!

No less than nineteen scholars of high repute for their commentaries or studies of the *Yh* have had their tablets erected in the Temple of Confucius.[1] These tablets are divided into four classes, viz.: 4 Associates, 12 Men of Genius, 79 Former Worthies, 66 Former Scholars. Among the 12 Men of Genius, the last is Chu Hi (1130-1200), the celebrated commentator, author of five works on the *Yh*, and of whom I spoke above. Among the 79 Former Worthies, the 9th is Shang Kiù (born 523 B.C.), above quoted; the 75th Chöu Tun-i (1017-1073); the 76th, Chang Tsai (1020-1076); the 78th, Ch'eng-I (1033-1107), author of a great commentary; the 79th, Shao Yung (1011-1077). Among the 66 Former Scholars, the 10th is Tu Tze Ch'ün (about B.C. 50-A.D. 40), a commentator; the 12th, Ch'eng Kang Ch'eng (A.D. 127-200), a commentator; the 14th, Fan Ning[2] (339-401); the 18th, Fan Chung-yen (989-1052); the 31st, Lü Tung-lai (1137-1181), author of a commentary; the 36th, Ts'ai Ch'en (1167-1230), author of speculations for divination by the numbers of the *Yh*; the 38th, Wei Liao-weng (1178-1237), author of a treatise on the *Yh*; the 40th, Wang Pai (1197-1274), author of a commentary;[3] the 43rd, Chao Fuh (1200-after 1251), who taught the *Yh* with the commentary on it by I-chu'an; the 44th, Hu Heng (1209-1281); the 46th, Wu Ch'eng (1247-1331), author of remarks on the *Yh*; the 53rd, Hü kü jen (died 1485); the 54th, Ts'ai Tsing (1453-1508), author of a treatise called *Yh-King Meng yn* 易經蒙引, which is chiefly a selection of notes and commentaries with original observations, and which, printed by Imperial order in 1529, has since remained a standard work on the *Yh*.[4] And

---

[1] See the excellent book of T. Watters, *A Guide to the Tablets in a Temple of Confucius*, Shanghai, 1879, 8vo.

[2] Fan Ning was opposed to magic and divination, and to all the vain heresies of his time; he wrote fiercely against Wang-Pi (above quoted), who during the preceding century had struck out a new system of divination for the *Yh*. See T. Watters, *O.C.* p. 107.

[3] See T. Watters, *O.C.* pp. 169 and 181.

[4] See T. Watters, *O.C.* p. 208, and pp. 28, 45, 66, 70, 76, 79, 97, 100, 107, 114, 147, 160, 167, 180, 181, 187, 205, and 207.

outside the temple, in the "Temple of Ancestors glorified as Sages," is the tablet[1] of Ts'ai Yuen-ting (1135-1198), celebrated for his erudition in general, and notably for his labours in elucidation of the text of the *Yh*.[2]

55. So little satisfaction was given by all these various schools or proposals of interpretation, and so inadequate were they to illustrate the few passages of the *Yh* which are by no means obscure, that this mysterious book is still avowedly not understood, and that we assist, now-a-days, at a most curious spectacle.[3] There are not a few Chinese of education, among those who have picked up some knowledge, in Europe or in translations of European works, of our modern sciences, who believe openly that all these may be found in their *Yh*. Electricity, steam-power, astronomical laws, sphericity of the earth, etc., are all, according to their views, to be found in the *Yh-King*; they firmly believe that these discoveries were not ignored by their sages, who have embodied them in their mysterious classic, of which they will be able to unveil the secrets when they themselves apply to its study a thorough knowledge of the modern sciences. It is unnecessary for any European mind to insist upon the childishness of such an opinion. Even in admitting, what seems probable, that the early leaders of the Bak people (*Pöh sing*) were not without some astronomical and mathematical principles, which have been long since forgotten, there is no possible comparison whatever between their rude notions and our sciences. The latter imply a parallel knowledge of mechanical and industrial arts to which the Chinese have always been complete strangers.

[1] See T. Watters, *O.C.* p. 252.
[2] See Mayer, *C.R.M.* part i. n. 754.
[3] P. Gaubil, *Traité de la Chronologie Chinoise*, p. 81, writes of the *Yh-King* that " the different parts which compose this book do not give any fixed chronology. Not that there have not been Chinese who pretended that they found a chronology in the Y-King, and even in the eight Kwa, but there is no foundation to be made in these Chinese systems of chronology which are based on the Y-King, for those persons have made an Y-King according to their own fashion."—Thomas Fergusson, *Chinese Researches*, Part I. *Chinese Chronology and Cycles* (Shanghai, 1880, 12mo.), pp. 24-25. This little book, made up of quotations, would have been valuable, had the author displayed more discrimination in the choice of his authors. Simple reviewers, literary essayists, and mere dreamers, are credited with the same authority as scholars and specialists.

VI.—THE EUROPEAN INTERPRETATIONS.

56. The European scholars in their translations, or attempts at translations, have not yet reached this last stage. They are still behindhand or strangely in advance. Many have written and speculated on the Kwas, but few have attempted the hard task and responsibility of getting up a version. Several illustrious Jesuits have translated fragments of the work. P. Premare has translated the first two chapters with their appendices.[1] The 15th chapter has been translated twice, once by P. Couplet and others,[2] and once by the great P. Visdelou.[3] They have considered the heading 謙 *Kien* of this chapter as the real one, with the meaning *humility*, and have translated accordingly. Unhappily for the work done, the genuine object of the chapter is 兼 instead of 謙, so that all the interpretation built upon the latter falls to the ground.

57. We leave entirely aside the European speculations of the Kwas which cover a large ground, in almost every direction, magic, mystic philosophy, mathematics, natural philosophy, cosmogony, etc., and even music.[4] Cosmogony holds the first rank, as far as number of supporters is concerned, such views being those of many commentators; but, as Dr. J. Edkins has rightly remarked, there is no cosmogony in these symbols; and we can say that there is no connexion whatever between the contents of the chapters and the symbolism attached to the hexagrams. In our opinion there is a connexion still to be explained, between the hexagrams and the

---

[1] *Notes critiques pour entrer dans l'intelligence de l' Y-King* (Bibl. Nat. Fonds Chinois, No. 2720), by P. de Premare.
[2] In *Confucius Sinarum philosophus*, Paris, 1687.
[3] *Notice du Livre Chinois nommé Y-King, ou Livre canonique des changements*, avec des notes, by M. Claude Visdelou, Evêque de Claudiopolis, in the *Chou-King*, edit. P. Gaubil (1770), pp. 399-436. Reprinted in G. Pauthier's *Livres sacrés de l'Orient*, pp. 137-149. It had been written in 1728.
[4] An enumeration is found in H. Wuttke, *Die Entstehung der Schrift* (Leipzig, 1875, 8vo.), pp. 247, 748, and in Henri Cordier, *Bibliotheca Sinica*, vol. i. coll. 645-647. The two complete one another. Special papers or notes have been written by Martini, Leibnitz, P. Amiot, De Guignes, J. Klaproth, Abel Remusat, Seyffarth, W. Schott, G. Pauthier, J. Edkins, J. Haas, R. A. Jamieson, T. MacClatchie, Saint Martin, etc. *Vid.* also Neumann, in *Z. d. D. M. G.*, 1853, vii. 2, p. 144.

notched sticks of old, as expression of numbers and their use in belomancy.

In their speculations on the *Kwas* and the appended text, several German scholars are conspicuous for the special attention they have paid to the matter. We shall mention the old Mr. J. P. Schumacher,[1] of Wölfenbuttel, in 1763, who fancied that the Y-King was nothing else than a history of the Chinese.[2] Dr. O. Piper (1849–53), in two papers,[3] has considered it as the groundwork of a treatise on ethics in connection with the weak and strong lines of the hexagrams. Herr Adolf Helfferich (1868)[4] has indulged himself in worthless speculations on symbolism and linguistics on the first thirty chapters of the Yh; in somewhat nebulous explanations he holds that the Kwas are the basis of the Chinese writing and are somehow connected with the system of the knotted cords or Quippos.

We shall have disposed of the fragmentary translations in mentioning the work of P. A. Zottoli, of the present day (Nankinese Mission), who has published[5] a translation of a few chapters and almost all the appendices; the learned Jesuit was too great a sinologist to translate the text according to the farcical treatment of many Chinese commentators, and has displayed a praiseworthy wisdom in refusing to translate what cannot be translated, and being satisfied with few examples.

58. P. Regis and others have written on the whole text and commentaries a Latin version[6] of great brevity and excessive literalness, made with the help of the Manchu version. They have considered each row of characters as a

[1] *Die verborzenen Alterthümer der Sinesen aus dem uralten Kanonischen Y-King untersuchet*, von M. Joh. Heinrich Schumacher, Wölfenbüttel, 1763, 8vo. pp. 208.
[2] *Vid.* Wuttke, *Die Entstehung der Schrift*, p. 247.
[3] *Ueber das I-King. Die texte der Confucius welche sich auf die verschiedenen Reihenfolgen des Kwa beziehen* in Zeitschrift d. D. M. G., 1853, vii. pp. 187–214. —*Ueber das I-King, Die verschiedener Bestandtheile des Buche u. ihre Verstandlichkeit*, ibid. iii. 1849, pp. 273–301; v. 1851, pp. 195–220.
[4] *Turan und Iran. Ueber die Entstehung der Schriftsprache*, Frankfurt-à-M. 1868, 8vo. pp. 184. (*Das Chinesische I-King*, pp. 108–184).
[5] *Cursus litteraturæ linguæ sinica*, vol. iii. 1880.
[6] *Y-King*, Antiquissimus Sinarum liber (written about 1736) quem ex latina interpretatione P. Regis aliorumque ex Soc. Jesu P.P. edidit Julius Mohl. 2 vol. 1834, Stuttgard, 8vo.

current text, but were driven to render it in broken and short sentences. They have accepted bodily, without any inquiry into its antiquity and genuineness, the rather modern tradition attributing the authorship of the text to Wen Wang and Chöu Kung, and of the appendices to Confucius. Having so fettered themselves at the very outset, they have received as genuine the few sentences where allusions to personal affairs of Wen Wang have been supposed; and this led them to assume that the text relates to the transactions between the founders of the Chöu dynasty and the last sovereign of the Yn dynasty, and is, thus, capable of being historically illustrated. The result has been to impress upon their minds ideas of meanings which have nothing to do with the original text; but as they were sinologists of great attainments, they have given their views on the question of veiled allusions in their running commentaries, while honestly translating the text separately word for word. Their version, however, was done on the modern *Kiai-shu* text, as amended and modified by successive transcriptions in the manner we have pointed out. And as they have not taken into account the ancient meanings of the characters, the result is unsatisfactory, and utterly unintelligible. The inexactitude of the views they have taken is exploded by their version itself.[1]

59. The Rev. T. MacClatchie, of Shanghai, has published, in 1876, a complete English version, to which several allusions are made in the present paper. The learned missionary has not made any inquiries as to the origin and growth of the book. He has not distinguished the text from the appendices, and gives those which are intermingled with the text, as they are in the ordinary Chinese edition. He wanted to find in the Yh-King references to a cosmogony, based on the male and female principle of nature, and he has translated accordingly with Chinese commentators.[2]

---

[1] Dr. Legge (*Yi-King*, Preface, p. xv): "But their version is all but unintelligible, and mine was (?) not less so."

[2] *A translation of the Confucian* 易 經 *or the "Classic of Change," with notes and Appendix*, Shanghai, 1876, 8vo. The same author had published *The symbols of the Yh-King* (*China Review*, vol. i. pp. 151-163); *Phallic Worship* (ibid. vol. iv. pp. 257-261).

60. M. P. D. F. Philastre, who has acquired during a long stay in the East a good practical knowledge of the Chinese, has undertaken a complete version which will appear in the *Annales du Musée Guimet*, vols. vi. vii. He has already given, a few years ago, a foretaste of his views in his curious book called *La Genèse du Langage et du Mystère Antique*. Here we see that the Yh-King is more mystic than anything else in the world; the speculations of the most abstruse metaphysics are not so deep as the mysteries embodied, according to this writer, in the Chinese book. The symbolism of astronomy, electricity, chemistry, etc., is carried to the extreme, and discovered in every separate and individual consonant, vowel and accent composing the sound of each Chinese character, rendered in the Latin alphabet according to the French pronunciation and transcription!

The following extract will give an idea of the result:—
"*Premier diagramme, ou Koua*, Khièn=raisonnement sur (') le mouvement du soleil autour de la terre cause de conviction sur (k) l'éclat (h) obscurci de la lune et la (n) lumière du soleil." (sic!) [1]

The *Mystère Antique* (?) finds here its home, and the author thinks that he can illuminate this deep abyss. Speculations of this kind are beyond the limits of scientific research, and having no other ground than the imagination of the writer, are altogether foreign to our studies.

61. Now we come to the English paraphrase, not translation, lately published in the *Sacred Books of the East*, by Dr. J. Legge, the well-known author of valuable editions and translations (according to the commentaries) of several of the Chinese Classics.

The writer believes in the tradition of the authorship of the text by Wen Wang and Chöu Kung, and has endeavoured to justify it, but as the two quotations he gives, upon which this assertion rests, have proved (above §§ 14, 16, 17) not to bear this meaning, we have to consider it as a mere opinion which he has failed to support with satisfactory reasons. He

---

[1] Vid. P. D. F. Philastre, *Premier essai sur la Genèse du langage et la Mystère Antique* (Paris, 1879, 8vo.), p. 53.

rightly refuses to accept the part of this tradition which concerns the authorship of Confucius, but then why accept the first part? In disconnecting the text from the commentaries, as a necessary preliminary step to any understanding of the book, Dr. Legge follows the principle we had maintained previously.

With the prejudiced views of Wen Wang's and Chöu Kung's authorship of the text, Dr. Legge has, on the other hand, been strongly impressed by (1) the moral interpretations of Chu-hi; (2) the views of the Han scholars considering the book as a work of divination; and (3) the ideas of the first commentaries perpetuated by a long line of successors, to the effect that the system of symbolism of the strong and weak lines of the hexagram is followed in the sentences of the text. He has *combined the information*, and looking all along for allusions of these kinds, he has written an unintelligible paraphrase of each line of the text.

62. According to his views " the subject-matter of the text may be briefly represented as consisting of sixty-four short essays, enigmatically and symbolically expressed, on important themes, mostly of a moral, social and political character, and based on the same number of lineal figures, each made up of six lines, some of which are whole and the others divided."[1]

These imaginary essays and their internal adaptation to the strong and weak lines (undivided and divided) must of course be made to match with the views of the adaptor; and it is quite curious to see how the simple principle of the weak and strong lines system is distorted, with the view of making it correspond to the guessed meanings of the artificial phrases when they disagree too obviously. Such a method is undeserving the attention of a man of common sense; it is a compilation of guesses and suggestions, a monument of nonsense.

63. Going through the interpretations of the *Yh*, as proposed by the Chinese themselves, and of which the late English paraphrase is a fair specimen, one cannot fail to be

---

[1] *Vid.* Legge, *Yi-King*, Introduction, p. 10.

struck by the stupendous effort it represents. It shows plainly all that has been done by the tortured minds of the Chinese, all the fancies of their maddened brains in their attempts to understand what could not be understood. We do not know really which is the greater wonder, the marvellous patience of a hundred generations of Chinamen in piling up distorted and fantastic interpretations, and building this extraordinary Babel of nonsense and ingenuity, or the courage of European scholars who believe in it and present the achievement of such an interpretation as a *bona fide* written book.

64. The so-called sixty-four essays comprising the *Yh-King* text are, as we have said, fantastic creations, the protracted work of generations of interpreters. If we remember what we have said several years ago, that the greatest number of these chapters are nothing but mere lists of the different meanings of the leading character which is the subject of each chapter, it is easy to conceive that several of these meanings are often connected, when they are the natural extension by the evolution of ideas of the primitive meaning. This connection is the explanation of the delusion under which so many interpreters of the *Yh* have laboured.

By a constant strain on the meaning of the characters and the help given to that strain by the addition of the ideographical determinatives, especially at the times of the reforms of writing, and a non-interrupted pressure on the connection of the text with the lines of the hexagram, the Chinese interpreters have succeeded in forcing upon the text, in numerous cases, appearances of meaning. But these shadowy meanings are unavoidably disconnected, and to admit that they match one with another, within and beyond the limits of each chapter, requires an amount of goodwill and oblivion of all previous notions on the meanings of the characters, which cannot be reasonably granted.

65. It is impossible to believe that a man, in his sober senses, has ever written such foolish things as those which the interpreters followed by Dr. Legge invite us to accept; and on the hypothesis, not of the authorship which we dis-

prove, but of the arrangement of the text by Wen Wang which we believe, we have to choose between two opinions,— either that he was of unsound mind, not the sage so highly praised by all the Chinese traditions, and that his confinement at Yu-Li had affected his intellectual power, or, what is more likely, that he did not understand the whole of the old slips he had in his hands. Occasional gleams of sense, and rectifications made very likely by himself, confirm the great probability of our explanation.

If Wen Wang had written the *Yh* for the purpose which later interpreters have attributed to him, how is it that the sages who wrote the appendices have not been able to agree on this point? This is a very serious objection against all interpretations based upon such a theory.

VII.—Comparison of the Interpretations.

66. The number of special meanings and readings of characters in the *Yh-King*, suggested by commentators and adopted by interpreters, is enormous. In the greatest number of cases they have been made up for the occasion, and their *raison-d'être* is obvious. It was considered an absolute necessity to make them mean something *en rapport* with the other characters, and with a more or less far-fetched allusion to a good or bad, strong or weak fact, in connexion with the strong and weak lines. Their meanings have grown into currency by the process usual in such cases; suggested by one, quoted by another, repeated by a third, the meaning gains ground and thus at last becomes the *received* interpretation. Taking into account the general insufficiency of critical minds amongst the Chinese, this is the explanation required for the understanding what has happened in a great number of cases.[1]

[1] We do not intend by this remark to give any support to the views of a great geographer, Dr. J. Bretschneider of Peking, when in his paper on Chinese geography (*Notes and Queries*, vol. iv. p. 4) he says: "My opinion is that the Chinese of the present day are nearly idiots and incapable of a sensible critique." My learned friend Dr. Bushell (*The Chinese Recorder*, Aug. 1871, p. 63, where I find the quotation) has already protested against so sweeping an appreciation. The great lack of the Chinese critics is the absence of the sense of perspective and comparative method, and their defect is to accept too easily anything said of

The influence of these interpretations has been great on the successive transcriptions of the text and wings, before they had been crystallized in the modern style of writing. All the substitutions, alterations and augmentations of the characters of which we have spoken in previous sections of this paper could be quoted here to exemplify these remarks. But the pressure on the characters has not always been accompanied by the modification required, and many curious examples of the results obtained could here be quoted.

67. As an illustration of what we are pointing out, we shall indicate the treatment which one of the simplest and commonest Chinese characters has been made to undergo. In the 38th chapter, which consists of a vocabulary of the character 癸 (and not 暌 as written in modern writing), the third line runs as follows: 見與曳. 其牛掣. 其人. 天且劓.[1] etc., which are nothing more than five different meanings of 癸:

1. To see (*cf.* the modern character ideo-phonetic 暌).
2. To draw a chariot (*cf.* 駥).
3. An ox yoke.
4. It is in the Heavens (an opposition, *e.g.* of Sun and Moon, *cf.* 暌).
5. To slit the nose (*cf.* 劓).

It will scarcely be believed that in the commentaries 天 *T'ien* 'Heaven' has been interpreted by SHAVING ! ! ![2] and

---

old. But we Europeans have acquired our scientific methods only through many generations, and what was the western critic previous to this immense progress? I am not sure whether a considerable part of our western literature, even of the last few years, might not be judged by terms nearly as severe as those of the Russian physician.

[1] By a confusion of characters 人 is sometimes written instead of 入.

[2] *Vid. K'ang-hi tze Tien,* s.v. 天. It is interesting to see the efforts of commentators to make out this interpretation which occurs only once in Chinese literature, and this single case is this very passage of the Yh. Chu Hi and others have supposed that 天 has been written instead of 而, because of a certain resemblance of shape of the two characters in the *Chuen* style of writing, and that 而 'whiskers,' should represent 刪 'to shave the whiskers.' But this is impossible in palæography, as the latter is a compound character made for this meaning; 而 could have an affirmative and not a negative meaning of the existence of its object. The older commentators, most likely by homophony with 尖, had suggested "to prickle the face, to mark the forehead." *Vid.* the dictionaries 字彙, 正字通, 經籍籑詁 K. 16.

this has been accepted by P. Regis, Canon MacClatchie, and Dr. Legge, without the slightest remark.

P. Regis translates: "Visum currum detinet; ejus boves moratur; illius hominis capillos radit; nasum proscindit. . ." Dr. Legge translates: "In the third line, divided, we see one whose carriage is dragged back, while the oxen in it are pushed back, and he is himself subjected to the shaving of his head and the cutting off of his nose. . . ." (13 Chinese words = 40 English!)

68. Some of these made-up interpretations are amusing enough to dispel the spleen. For example, in the eighth chapter, again a vocabulary, we have the meanings of 比. This character signifies mainly "to compare," "to put in juxtaposition," thence to be near, though separated, and by the natural extension of ideas it has been applied to the crack in a vase.[1] Although this secondary meaning does not seem to occur in several of the other classics, we have the proof that it is a very old one by the expression "cracked earthenware" 比 輔 in the Siang chuen of the same chapter.

The rows 2, 3 and 4 of the characters in the text describe this meaning of the word as applied to a crack, in the following terms:—[2]

6-2—比 之 自 內 'cracked from inside.'
6-3—比 之 匪 入 'cracked, but not through.'[3]
6-4—外 比 之 'cracked outside.'

In P. Regis's translation,[4] where meanings are attempted with the help of the Manchu version with but very few additions to the text, we find respectively:—

2—Ex intimis inire fœdus.
2—Si, qui fœdus init.
4—Ad extra fœdus init.

Taking now the late English version, we immediately reach

---

[1] With this meaning it is now written 比皮, 比攴.
[2] We neglect the fore-telling words 貞 吉 added to the second and fourth sentences.
[3] The last character of 6-3 is sometimes written 人 by a confusion with 入, but the parallelism of the three sentences do not allow of any mistake in translating.
[4] See vol. i. pp. 323, 325, 327.

the height of fancy in the following phrases which are given as the translation of the seventeen Chinese characters above:—

2. "In the second line, divided, we see the movement towards union and attachment proceeding from the inward (mind)."

3. "In the third line, divided, we see its subject seeking for union with such as ought not to be associated with."

4. "In the fourth line, divided, we see its subject seeking for union with the one beyond himself."[1]

Altogether fifty-seven English words for seventeen Chinese. And what a galimatias! What a marvel of tortured ingenuity! One is led to think that the native interpreters could not understand the crack in the text because of the crack in their brain.

69. So little reliance can be placed upon the translations hitherto published that it is difficult to find the same passage translated by two sinologists in an identical manner. And what is more curious is to see the same passages translated differently by the same scholar, as for example, passages quoted in the *Tso Chuen* translated there and afterwards differently in the version of the *Yh*. This is almost conclusive, and shows what a monument of fancy are the interpretations as last given to the *Yh*. But we do not want to find fault with one sinologist more than with another; it is not the individual work we are attacking, but the methods which have been followed.

We shall give a few examples of the discrepancies of translation. In the *Tso Chuen*, 1st year of Duke Chao (541 B.C.), there is a quotation from the *Yh* of Chöu.[2] The words chosen are taken from the second wing, the *Siang* (which is never quoted when the *Yh* of Chöu is not specified),

---

[1] See Legge, *Yi-King*, pp. 74, 75.
[2] The quotation from the second wing, as well as others of the same kind, show unmistakably that those wings (1st and 2nd) were considered as integral parts of the *Yh* of Chöu, and intermingled with the text. The tradition attributing the intermingling to Fei-Chi, or more likely to Tien Ho, is not very clear, and from an examination of the list extracted from the 'Former Han Records,' as well as from the quotation here noticed, it seems that the two arrangements, namely with and without, were equally adopted. *Vid.* above, § 47.

and from the 18th chapter: 風落山 "the wind falls on the mountain," which is translated in Dr. Legge's version of the *Tso Chuen*: "the wind throwing down (the trees of a) mountain."[1] In the present *Yh-King*, we find the sentence written as follows: 山下有風 "The foot of the mountain is windy," which in Dr. Legge's version of the *Yh* is translated: "(The trigram for) a mountain and below is that for wind, from Kû"!!! (Kû is the name for the Kwa).[2]

70. In the *Tso-Chuen*, 1st year of Duke Ch'ao, § 10. 2,[3] we read, according to Dr. Legge, that the *Yh* of Chöu under the symbol 蠱, speaks of *a woman deluding a young man* 女惑男. Here we have the meaning assigned at that period to the beginning of the second line: 幹母之蠱; the same sentence which we find translated in P. Regis's version by "*curam habet infortunii matris*,"[4] and in Dr. Legge's late version: "The second line, undivided, *shows (a son) dealing with the troubles caused by his mother.*"[5]

Which of these three versions is correct? The last must be erroneous, because there is in it much more than the four Chinese characters can support. To choose between the meanings as given in the *Tso-Chuen* and the Regis version, would be a difficult task, but we are saved the trouble when we remember that the character 蠱 is one of those which Wen Wang has substituted, and that the old one was 胤.[6] Having discovered the proper character we are unable to find the proper meanings, and the whole chapter when translated, without introducing any theories or far-fetched ideas, resolves itself into a mere list of the meanings of the said character.

71. We cannot help recognizing that such, amusing as they may be, systems of translation are a dangerous game to play at, since they open the way to all the imprudences of imagination. Such a method, followed by several persons equally trained to its pursuit, cannot fail to produce the

---

[1] *Vid. Chinese Classics*, vol. v. p. 581.
[2] *Vid. Sacred Books of the East*, vol. xvi. p. 291.
[3] *Chinese Classics*, edit. Legge, vol. v. pp. 574, 581.
[4] *Y-King*, vol. ii. p. 16.
[5] *The Sacred Books of the East*, vol. xvi. p. 95.
[6] See above, § 39.

widest divergences in the case of almost every single passage.[1] So we have in the *Yh*, Chap. XVIII. 1-6, 幹 父 之 蠱, which, translated as a phrase, gives, according to

Dr. Wells Williams,[2] "To follow a father's calling";

Dr. Legge,[3] "A son dealing with the trouble caused by his father";

P. Regis,[4] "Curam habet infortunii patris."

72. But this example is nothing compared with the strange phenomena we have quoted. We refer to the obvious proof given by the translation of the *Yh-King* by Canon Mac-Clatchie, who has followed a method of his own, and has been able to produce a version consistent from beginning to end, but evidently wrong from its very departure. We have again an example of the consequences of the same process in the fragmentary translations of the *Yh* published by the French scholar, M. E. Philastre, whose ground is an obscure mysticism and symbolism, and is vitiated by the same radical fallacy throughout. And if we compare with these two the elegant but unintelligible translation lately published by Dr. Legge, we cannot fail to recognize the same inherent defect, with this difference, however, that the systematic views to which he has bent his translation are not properly his own, but only the consummation of the Chinese theories he has adopted from many commentators of the book.

VIII.—Methods of Interpretation.

73. That the question of method is of primary importance in dealing with such a work as the *Yh* does not require any kind of demonstration.

We have seen that the classification, emendation, and rectification of the old slips or rows of characters, addition of many foretelling words, with an attempt at their adapta-

---

[1] *Cf.* below, the translations of P. Regis, Rev. MacClatchie, and of Dr. Legge, §§ 90, 93, 95, 97, 99, and 101.
[2] *Syllabic Dictionary*, p. 434.
[3] *The Yi-King*, p. 95.
[4] *Y-King*, vol. ii. p. 14.

tion to the strong and weak lines, or perhaps only to the upper and lower trigram of the hexagram, were in all probability the work of Wen Wang,[1] who wrote the commentary *Twan* which follows the first line of every chapter. The task was continued by his son Chöu Kung in his commentary *Siang* which follows the *Twan*, and each of the six lines of every chapter, where he attempts to interpret the meanings.

74. The author of the wing, the *Sü Kwa* 序卦, whoever he may have been, seems to have come very near understanding some parts of the text. But it is obvious that he was in some way fettered by the previous commentaries of Wen Wang and Chöu Kung. Moreover he could not conceive a fact so simple as the real one, namely, that the book is composed of mere lists of meanings of characters. Instead of looking to each chapter for the meanings of the character which heads it, he sought for its sound as it was at his time and place, and he has enumerated the meanings of its homophones.

The same process was partly employed by Wen Wang, and more extensively by Chöu Kung, and was continued in the commentaries after the time of the author of the *Sü Kwa*; many interpretations have been suggested by, and handed down from the early commentators by meanings suggested to them by homophones at their time and in their dialects, with the temporary phonetic equivalents: K=T, P=K, M=P, NG=T-K, Y=S, Sh=L, L=K, etc. This interesting feature, which is the clue to many curious suggestions, is inherent in the phonetic history of the language, as will be pointed out at its occurrence in my version.

75. The *Yh-King* has never been lost and found again more or less incomplete, as was the case with the *Shu-King* and the *Shi-King*, and was not, like them, exposed to losses and misreading under the process of decipherment. But it was subject in the fullest degree to all the inconveniences of transcribing the text in the new styles of writing, especially at the time of the Literary Revival under the Han period.

---

[1] A fact, began certainly previously to his time.

Many passages of a dubious meaning have been crystallized into a more determinate interpretation through the transcription in a more ideographic style of writing. In the case of a text which, as the appendices show, was so difficult to understand, it is obvious that the addition to the characters of ideographic determinatives (vulg. the keys) precising their meaning, was a matter which depended entirely on the exactitude of the interpretation, and was altogether valueless if, as we know, the interpretation was often misunderstood.

76. We have seen in previous §§ (38–41) how long the process of substitution and modification of characters of the text had been going on, and from the numerical importance of these changes and additions we are able to appreciate how widely an exact transcription of the old text in Kiai shu (modern) strokes would have differed from the text as we now possess it. The original has been gradually modified by the transcribers in accordance with suggestions of meanings by the commentators, and significations obtained by a factitious and persistent pressure of the mind in search of allegories and tropes of speech. Such meanings were considered as satisfactory when they appeared to be supported by a temporary and local homonymy, in connection with the supposed thesis of the chapter and its division according to the strong and weak lines.

Notwithstanding these protracted exertions, how poor is the result! How disconnected are the meanings! What extraordinary fancies! How unreasonable it all is! It has been impossible to find any continuity in the chapters individually or in the series. All the efforts of the interpreters have proved fruitless, and the attempts of the late English translator result in total failure.

77. We have not here to consider the systems sought for in the *Yh*, which have had a great influence on the proposed meanings. Enough has been said of the native interpretations, and in what concerns the European ones, we are bound to recognize that such systematic views have had very little if any influence on P. Regis's version (leaving aside his commentaries), but, on the contrary, have strongly

swayed the versions of Canon MacClatchie, Mr. Philastre, and the paraphrase of Dr. Legge.

The *acmé* of these processes of interpretation is to be found in the *guess-at-the-meaning* principle of translation, of which the eminent missionary-Professor is a staunch supporter. He has endeavoured to justify his process of paraphrasing instead of literally translating, by the most obnoxious system ever found in philology. If this easy process were to be henceforth followed, as unhappily seems to be the case in recent translations, it would be destructive of all trustworthiness in any translation. In Dr. Legge's hands we are afraid this system has proved a very unsafe instrument. The learned sinologist thought he could trust it even in the case of an untranslatable text, because it had rendered him good service and facilitated his task in many passages of his translations of several of the other Chinese classics, where the context, the sequence of facts and ideas and the commentaries supported it.

78. Let us inquire in what consists this *guess-at-the-meaning* method, and on what ground it rests. "The great thing," we are told,[1] "is to get behind and beyond the characters, till one comes into *rapport* and sympathy with the original speakers and relaters." "We must try with our thoughts to meet the scope of a sentence, and then we shall apprehend it."[2] "In the study of a Chinese classical book, there is not so much an interpretation of the characters employed by the writer as a participation of his thoughts; there is the seeing of mind to mind."[3]

It is obvious that all this opens a door to any fancy of a translator, who will always easily imagine, in perfect good faith, that his mind (in its wanderings?) has seen the mind of the author he interprets. We must protest energetically against such a demoralizing doctrine, which would be the ruin, by the facility it presents, of all those who have the duty of translating any Chinese book. We should no longer

---

[1] By Dr. J. Legge, in his paper on the *Principles of Composition in Chinese, as deduced from the Written Characters*, in J.R.A.S. Vol. XI. n.s. 1879, p. 255.
[2] *Vid.* his Preface to the *Yi-King*, p. xx.
[3] *Ibid.*

be able to trust any translation without first comparing it word for word with the original. All confidence in the work of others, which is so necessary a factor in literary research, would be destroyed. By this system, the same text translated by two different persons will never give the same rendering; and, proofs in hand, we may say more, viz. the same text translated by the same person in two different moments will not be rendered with the same sense.

79. The written characters are the vehicle of the thought of a writer, and it is by an attentive study of these characters, their individual meanings, their place in a sentence, and the place of the sentence in the context, and by this only, that we can know what he meant, and express it in another tongue. The "meeting of the scope," "the seeing of mind to mind," are charming poetical expressions, but they have nothing to do, in that case, with a sound scholarship. Any one who translates a text must never forget that he has in his hands a *fidei commissum*, and that he will commit a breach of trust, in every case where he exposes himself to write his own views instead of those of his author.

80. The method of *guessing-at-the-meaning* is said to have been taught by the old Chinese philosopher Mencius (B.C. 372–289),[1] who laid down some such principles, in what concerns the 'Book of Poetry,' and that book only, because of the metaphors and figures of speech familiar to poets, and which are not to be taken literally, but as explained by the context.

We reproduce the whole section (as a part of it would not carry the same meaning), according to the translation of Dr. Legge,[2] as follows:

"Hien-k'ew Mung said, 'On the point of Shun's not treating Yaou as a minister, I have received your instructions. But it is said in the Book of Poetry,

    'Under the whole heaven
    Every spot is the sovereign's ground;
    To the borders of the land,
    Every individual is the sovereign's minister';

---

[1] *Vid.* bk. v. pt. ii. ch. iv. § 2.
[2] *Vid.* The *Chinese Classics*, vol. ii. pp. 228, 229.

and Shun had become emperor. I venture to ask how it was that Koo-sow was not one of his ministers.'¹ *Mencius* answered, " That ode is not to be understood in that way ; it speaks of being laboriously engaged in the sovereign's business, so as not to be able to nourish one's parents, *as if the author* said, ' This is all the sovereign's business, and *how is it that* I alone am supposed to have ability, and am made to toil in it ? ' Therefore those who explain the odes, may not insist on one term so as to do violence to a sentence, nor on a sentence so as to do violence to the general scope. They must try with their thoughts to meet that scope, and then we shall apprehend it. If we simply take single sentences, there is that in the ode called ' The Milky Way,' ²

' Of the black-haired people of the remnant of Chow,
There is not half a one left.' ³

If it had been really as thus expressed, then not an individual of the people of Chow was left."

Comparing these two quotations from the *Shi-King* with the strophes from which they are extracted, and the explanations of the chatty Mencius, it is obvious that he has only pointed out that the poetical expressions of the Shi-King are not to be taken literally in mangled quotations. He has not laid down principles for the elucidation of all the classics, and in any case his principles have nothing to do with the *guess-at-the-meaning* principle.

---

¹ The whole strophe runs as follows (pt. ii. bk. vi. od. i. st. 2) : " Under the wide heaven,—All is the king's land.—Within the sea boundaries of the land,—All are the king's servants.—The great officers are unfair,—Making me serve thus as if I alone were worthy." - Legge, *Chinese Classics*, vol. iv. pp. 360, 361. The writer means that as every one is equally at the sovereign's disposal, it is unfair for his great officers to make him serve, as if he was the only one to do it.

² Dr. Legge has taken these two phrases, beginning from " not insist," and ending " apprehend it," as motto of his translations, vols. ii. iii. iv. v., but he has omitted the beginning, " Therefore those who explain the Odes," so that his mangled quotation does not carry the meaning intended by Mencius.

³ The whole strophe runs as follows (pt. iii. bk. iii. od. iv. st. 3) : " The drought is excessive,—And I may not try to excuse myself.—I am full of terror and feel the peril,—Like the clap of thunder or the roll.—Of the remnant of Chow among the black-haired people,—There will not be half a man left ;—Nor will God from His great heaven—Exempt (even) me. . . ." *Vid.* Legge, *Chinese Classics*, vol. iv. p. 530. The author apprehends future evils if the drought continues longer.

81. The views which I have disputed (§§ 77, 78), have been conceived under a grave delusion in regard to the old Chinese style. To hold that the written characters of the Chinese are not representations of words but symbols of ideas, and that the combination of them in composition is not a representation of what the writer would say, but of what he thinks,[1] is rather an exaggeration. It is only partially true of the book-language of to-day, which is nothing else but an abridgment, more ideographic than phonetic, of the spoken language with the extensive ornamentation in literary style of idioms borrowed from literature, history, etc. But the wide gap which exists now between the colloquial and the written language has not always existed. It has been widened and deepened progressively. At first the written language was the faithful phonetic reproduction of the spoken one. So true is this, that with the help of the laws of orthography of the period, we can transcribe the few old fragments we possess from their pure Ku-wen characters into modern ones, and that they correspond exactly to the spoken language. There are still indications of this remarkable fact, in the oldest chapters of the *Shu-King*, through their transcriptions down to the modern form of characters. This early style was subsequently modified, and the assertion of Remusat, inferred from the modern characters, that the Ancient style was sententious, vague, concise and disconnected, is not to be accepted without reserve. The ancient predominance of phonetic characters, single and compound, has gradually yielded place to a preponderance of ideograms. The official modification of writing by *She Chöu* about 820 B.C. for political purposes is a well-known fact. Once open, the gap has not only never been filled, but on the contrary has had an uninterrupted tendency to be widened by the continuous increase of literary idioms. Besides this, many words are still represented, in the book language, by characters of which the sound is now obsolete for the colloquial, the former having but seldom followed the phonetic decay of the latter, while

---

[1] *Vid.* Legge's *Preface* to his *Yi-King*, p. xv.

the modifications it has undergone during many centuries are very slight.

82. I hope that these lengthy discussions and explanations will be understood for what they are, viz. an attempt to define the situation, to clear the ground and justify the method I follow in my translation of the *Yh*.

It seems to me that it is mere waste of time to attempt a real and true version of the *Yh-King* without having laboured a good deal previously, in palæographical researches and linguistic studies, of which the European translators do not seem to have conceived the necessity and importance. A faithful version of the *Yh* is certainly not a matter of illumination, or inspiration, or of "meeting the scope" of the author. It can only be the result of patient and extensive researches. It cannot be obtained by the strained application of any preconceived theory, because the adaptation, classification and repetition, to which the text has been exposed, is obviously an after-arrangement, independent of what the text was originally. I repudiate altogether what I have called the *guess-at-the-meaning* principle as destructive of a true rendering, because the translator who follows it cannot help guessing "behind and beyond" the characters according to his prejudiced views. The attempt to translate the *Yh* by the *Yh*, *i.e.* by the idioms which have been introduced into literature from the supposed interpretation, is a danger which does not seem to have been hitherto perceived, and which I shall try to avoid. I translate literally, with no addition beyond what is required by the exigencies of grammar. This was the system followed by P. Regis, but he had not the help of palæography and linguistic studies. I desire to remain on the *terra firma* of scientific method, having found that, by this process, all extravagant and fantastic views are entirely ignored, and that a very simple and easily understood explanation of the text of the *Yh* is obtained. This old book has much more importance for the history of the Chinese language, writing, culture and people than has been supposed.

IX.—Translations from the Yh.

83. When considering the Chinese text of the *Yh-King*, as it now stands, the observer is struck with the frequent repetition throughout the book of a small number of different formulæ in one, two, or three words, the whole being obviously the foretelling words surreptitiously added by Wen Wang when he arranged, without understanding their real character, the ancient slips he had in hand.[1] There is no doubt that these words did occur here and there in the old texts, previously to Wen Wang's arrangement, and that he has mistaken their proper primary value in the context; he has considered them as foretelling words, and repeated them in every section of the book.

84. Such formulæ as 无咎, 无悔, 无吉, 貞吉, 終吉, 利 貞, which occur very often,[2] and 有 終, 有 孚, which are met with less frequently, are almost always foretelling words added afterwards; of course they have to be neglected in a translation bearing on the old text only. The formula 无 悔 [3] is sometimes uncertain, because the character 悔 has been substituted[4] for 卟 in all the cases where this last occurred in Wen Wang's text, and consequently cannot be distinguished any more from the cases where 悔 did occur previously in the genuine text. The oldest shape of 悔 was 毎 before Wen Wang's time.

85. A remark is also necessary on the character 利, which in the interpolated foretelling formula has the meaning of "benefit"; but the same form is the oldest one of 黎 "many, numerous," which did occur in the ancient text, but because the character has the other meaning of fortune telling, it was not recognized by the transcribers in modern style with its

---

[1] "He added and subreptitiously introduced the foretelling words, . . ." *Vid.* above, § 13, quotation (*i*).

[2] On an interesting coincidence presented by several of these foretelling words with Assyrian ones, *vid.* my *Early History of Chinese Civilization*, p. 26.

[3] 無 *wu* 'not' as used in the *Yh* is always written 无, a variation first introduced by the followers of Lao-tze and Chwang-tze. *Vid.* Tai Tung, *Luh shu Ku*; L. C. Hopkins, *The Six Scripts*, a translation (Amoy, 1881, 8vo.), p. 35.

[4] *Cf.* Min tsi Ki, *Luh shu tung*, K. vii. f. 48.

meaning of plurality, and in consequence not rewritten 黎, as it ought to have been.

Other foretelling words are 凶, 貞, 吉, etc., which occur very frequently and are evident interpolations. The same is most likely to be said of 元 "primary," "original," sometimes joined to one or two of the above quoted characters.

We have, moreover, to mention here 亨, which occurs about fifty times. It is placed in twenty-nine cases immediately after the character which forms the subject-matter of the chapter, and is ten times preceded by 元. It denotes "to pervade, to go through," and seeing that it precedes the enumeration of the various acceptations of the head-words of the chapter, it is this character we should have expected to find in order to suggest "meanings" or "significations," to which it corresponds plainly.

86. It might be useful to repeat once more that the result of our studies is that the *Yh-King* has been made up of various documents of very ancient date, of which the contents were forgotten, or misunderstood, and in consequence considered as a book of fate, for which purpose many foretelling words, according to the Chinese tradition, were subreptitiously introduced and interpolated in the old rows of characters.

87. In order to demonstrate all that has been stated and unravelled in the preceding pages, we must go through several chapters of this mysterious classic. As the vocabulary-chapters are the most numerous, we shall give the English version of a few of them, and then of a chapter in which is embodied an old ballad relating to an historical fact of the twenty-second century B.C. We shall conclude with an anthropological chapter speaking of Aboriginal Tribes.

This translation is not to be considered as definitive, and is very far from the comparative stage of completion to which it should be carried out. It is only an outline showing how the book has been made up and what materials are gathered in it. More precise meanings, in many cases, might be found in order to obtain more accuracy, and I dare say the result would be still more satisfactory in corresponding acceptations and meanings than those given below.

88. The choice of the seventh chapter was indicated to us as a specimen suitable to show the genuineness of our views about the vocabulary chapters, by the importance given to it by the last translator of the *Yh*, Dr. J. Legge. According to the Rev. Professor of Oxford, who has repeated his translation of the chapter in his Introduction as "a fair specimen" of what he calls "the essays that make up the Yî of *K*âu,"[1] "so would," he says, "King Wăn and his son have had all military expeditions conducted in their country 3000 years ago. It seems to me that the principles which they lay down might find a suitable application in the modern warfare of our civilized and Christian Europe. The inculcation of such lessons cannot have been without good effect in China during the long course of its history"[2] !!! No other result but insanity could be produced by this supposed essay, as well as by all the others which, as we said, are of the same kind; as our readers will judge, in the perusal of what is supposed by the said Professor to be the genuine meaning of the text. For this purpose we reproduce, in smaller type, his translation, with those of the Rev. MacClatchie and P. Regis, in parallel columns, juxtaposed to the English equivalents we give with the text. In an intermediary column, next to the Chinese text, and as a proof of the exactitude of our rendering, we have placed the characters in their ancient[3] and modern forms, which in the vocabularies are successively described.

The rendering of the foretelling words, as we have said above, is left blank.

89. Before passing to the rendering of the said chapter on 師, let us peruse the various acceptations of this word in those of the classics published in English by Dr. J. Legge, through the valuable indices he has framed for them.

---

[1] *Sacred Books of the East*, vol. xvi. Introd. p. 25 : "The subject-matter of the text may be briefly represented as consisting of sixty-four short essays, enigmatically and symbolically expressed, on important themes, mostly of a moral, social, and political character, and based on the same number of lineal figures, each made up of six lines, some of which are whole and the others divided." *Vid*. *ibid*. p. 10.
[2] *Ibid*. p. 25.
[3] Written in modern strokes, in Kiai-shu or pattern-writing, for the sake of convenience.

In the *Shu-King*,[1] we find the following acceptations :

(1) The multitudes, the people; all.—(2) A capital city.—(3) An army, a host.—(4) Instructors.—(5) Applied to various officers, . . . tutors, a high office appointed by Yu, . . . judges.—(6) A model, to take as a model.

In the *Shi-King* :[2]

(1) A multitude, all.—(2) Forces, troops.—(3) 京 師 the capital.—(4) Master.—(5) Various officers.—(6) To imitate.

In the *Chun Tsiu* :[3]

(1) An army, a force, etc.

In the "Great learning," the "Doctrine of the Mean" and the "Conversations of Confucius" :[4]

(1) The multitude, the people.—(2) A host.—(3) A teacher.—(4) Sundry officers, etc.

In Möng-tze (Mencius) :[5]

(1) A military host.—(2) A teacher, master.—(3) To make one's master, to follow.—(4) Sundry officers.

We will now proceed with the version :

[1] *Vid.* Legge's *Chinese Classics*, vol. iii. p. 672.
[2] Vol. iv. p. 711.
[3] Vol. v. p. 902.
[4] Vol. i. p. 333.
[5] Vol. ii. p. 429.

90.—The VIIth Chapter 師 Sze (A Vocabulary).

Text.	Our Version.			Other Versions Compared.		
	Characters described.		English.	P. Regis.	Rev. MacClatchie.	Dr. J. Legge.
	Old.	Modern.				
師貞丈人吉无咎	師 = 師 "a master."		Sze (is) a righteous great man. 0 0 0	Sze Solidum vir egregius; bonum sine ullo malo.	Sze implies Completion; using an eminent leader is now attended with luck, and no danger ensues.	Sze indicates how in the case which it supposes, with firmness and correctness and (a leader of) age and experience, there will be good fortune and no error.
上六大君有命開國承家小人勿用 律 凶	師 = id. "a judge."		(First 6.) The Sze defines laws not biassed.	Epiphona primum. Si milites exeant, leges sequantur. Si non bene, pessimum est.	First six. Represents the army coming forth and acting according to law; if it proves unfaithful then ill luck ensue.	The first line, divided, shows the host going forth according to the rules (for such a movement). If these be not good, there will be evil.

九二 在師中 吉无咎 王三錫命	師 = id. "the army." 師 = id. "officers."	(IX. 2.) The centre of the army. 0 0 0 The three conveying orders (officers) of the sovereign.[1]	Epiphona secundum. Est in medio militum. Bonum est. Nullum est malum Rex tria diversa mandata dedit.	Second nine. Is the army attaining the due medium, good luck follows; no blame arising, the sovereign will bestow frequent commendations upon them.	The second line, undivided, shows (the leader) in the midst of the host. There will be good fortune and no error. The king has thrice conveyed to him the orders (of his favour).
六三 師或輿尸 凶	師 = id. "passive multitude."	(6–3.) Sze (is) also corpse-like. 0	Epiphona tertium. Milites videntur deponere sarcinas in curribus. Male: seu, o infortunium.	Third six represents soldiers as it were lying dead in the baggage carts, and is unlucky.	The third line, divided, shows how the host may, possibly, have many inefficient leaders. There will be evil.
六四 師左次 无咎	師 = id. "the assistant music master."	(4–6.) Sze (is) an assistant officer. 0 0	In quartum sextum. Milites ad laeva castra metantur. Nullum est malum.	Fourth-six. Is the army retreating; no danger ensues.	The fourth line, divided, shows the host in retreat. There is no error.

[1] The three first acceptations do not require any observation, as they are quite plain. As to "the three conveying orders (officers) of the sovereigns," are we to understand the officers of the Three Rulers 三皇, Fuh-hi, Shen-ming and Hwang-ti, who each give them names relating to dragons, fire and clouds respectively? (Vid. *Tso Chuen*, Duke Chao, 17th year.) On the other hand, under the Shang dynasty, perhaps before, there were two classes of three officers, each beginning by a 師 greater or smaller, of which the generic names according to the *Shu-King* (Vid. Legge's edit. p. 274) were the "three Kung," and the three *Ku*. But in the 天元曆理 (quoted in G. Schlegel, *Uranographie Chinoise*, p. 528) the "three Kung" are called the "three Sze." The first suggestion is most probably the true one.

THE YIH-KING AND ITS AUTHORS.

		(6-5.)	In quintum sextum.	Fifth-six.	The fifth line divided, shows birds in the fields, which it will be advantageous to seize (and destroy). In that case there will be no error. If the eldest son leads the host and younger men (idly) occupy offices assigned to them) however firm and correct he may be, there will be evil.
六五 田有禽 利執言	師 = 鳥 "a large kind of sparrow."[1]	In the fields are birds (so called) many take the name.	Praedae sunt in campis, oportet loqui de illa capienda. Nullum est malum natu majoribus committere milites. Natu minores ad sarcinas adhibere, licet solidum, malum est.	Represents beasts in the field; there is benefit in catching and no danger ensues. The eldest son may now have a command in the army, but a younger son will lie dead in the baggage cart (if he joins it). Even when moral undeflectedness is preserved (this stroke) is unlucky.	
无咎 長子帥師	師 = 師 "leader of an army."	0 0 The elder sons (are) the leaders of the army.			
弟子輿尸	師 = id. "a passive host."	0 0 The younger (are) the passive multitude.			
貞凶					

[1] I do not give this suggestion without reluctance, because I have no proof whatever that the name *sze* for birds of a certain kind was ever used in ancient times. *Eo nomine* the name does not appear, as far as we know from the *Khang-hi Tze-tien* (*Puh* 50+10 strokes, f. 70v.), elsewhere before the *Poh wuh chi* (a work of the third century A.D.), quoting it as a bird also found in the T'iao ch'i 條支 State dynasty (Vid. *Tai P'ing yü lan*, K. 793, f. 1v.), and has been identified with the Tadjiks and Arabs in Persia... (Vid. E. Bretschneider, *On the Knowledge possessed by the Ancient Chinese of the Arabs and Arabian Colonies*, p. 6 and sq.). In the above case, which cannot be settled, as we have no positive proofs that *sze* was not used in relation with special birds, we may be satisfied of the positive assertion of the text that it was used in speaking of a large number of birds. The country is described in the Annals of the Han and Western Sea.

THE YH-KING AND ITS AUTHORS.

上六		(Upper 6.)		
大君有命	師 = id. "the grand teacher." 師 = id. "great officers."	Great prince instructing. The group of men who have helped at the organization of the kingdom.[1]	In sextum sextum. Exiit mandatum magni regis. Aperitregnum. Dat domos. Noli uti desipientio opera.	Sixth-six. The powerful Prince now bestows rewards, laying the foundation of the Dynasty, and appointing assistants in office; the inferior man is now useless.
開國承家				
小人勿用	師 = id. "multitude, crowd."	People gathered by the *wuh* flag.[2]		The topmost line, divided, shows the great ruler delivering his charges, appointing (some) to be rulers of states, and others to undertake the headships of clans; but small men should not be employed (in such positions).

[1] Here we have undoubtedly an allusion to the twelve *Sz* established by Yü over the twelve provinces at the time of the organization of the kingdom. (Vid. *Shu-King*, part ii. bk. iv. §8, Legge's edit. p. 85, Medhurst's edit. p. 75.)

[2] The *wuh* 勿 was a small flag with three pennons attached, which was hoisted by officials to call the people of a commune together; thence came the expression 勿勿 *wuh wuh* "make haste," according to the *Shwoh wen* (first cent.). Vid. *Khang-hi Tze-tien*, Pu 20+2 str. f. 68v.)

91. If the reader compares the description given in our version of the various acceptations of the word 師 *Sze* (made clear by the necessary remarks in the foot-notes, with the extracts of vocabularies of several classics on the same word which we have reproduced above (§ 89), he will be struck by the perfect correlation, and be satisfied that our statement is sound, viz. that the *Sze* chapter is made up of the slips containing the vocabulary describing the word. All the remarks, which we have to make of unavoidable length, are *mutatis mutandis*, applicable to the other chapters.

92. The following chapter, of which we give the version, is the fifteenth relating to 兼, which has been completed later on by a determinative and written 謙, as we have reported above (§ 39) from an ancient tradition.

The use of this character, with the proper determinative, has been extended to a large number of acceptations, but in early times, the various meanings attached to it were rather small.[1] The author of the re-arrangement had therefore to repeat several of them, in order to fill up the required number of lines.

The most interesting feature is the quotation about the spoonbill or *Platalea major*, an interesting bird which occupies a large place in Chinese literature from an early period. It is described in the *Œl-ya, Shan Haï King*, and was "a strange bird like a duck, the paired-wing bird, with one eye and one wing, affiliated to the plaice in its structure, and so made that two must unite for either of them to fly." It is still found in Formosa.[2]

Here is the version of the chapter :

---

[1] They are only those represented by the character itself with the determinatives (or keys) 38, 43, 61, 85, 149, 154. Cf. Min tsi Ki, *Luh shu tung*, K. iv. ff. 67, 68 ; K. viii. f. 46.

[2] Vid. *Taï Ping yu lan*, K. 927, f. 2v. *Khang-hi Tze-tien*, Pu 196+10 str. f. 73. And also Wells Williams, *Syllabic Dictionary of the Chinese Language*, p. 382. Mr. Rob. Swinhoe had caught several of those birds at Tamsui, Formosa ; *vid.* a notice of his in *Notes and Queries on China and Japan*, vol. i. p. 131 (Oct. 31, 1867).

93.—The XVth Chapter 謙, Anciently 兼 (A Vocabulary).

Modernized Text.	Our Version.			Other Versions Compared.		
	Characters described.		English.	P. Regis.	Rev. MacClatchie.	Dr. J. Legge.
	Old. Modern.					
謙亨君子有終	兼 = 謙 "satisfaction of results."		Meanings of *Kien*. Princely (good) issue.	Kien est penetrans. Sapiens finem habet.	The Kheen diagram implies luxuriance. The model man obtains the (advantage of) it throughout his life	*Khien* indicates progress and success. The superior man (being humble as it implies) will have a (good) issue to his undertakings.
上六謙君子用涉大川吉	兼 = 謙 "join together."		(Upper 6.) To join together, as do the princes when passing over the river.	Epiphona primum. Humilitati humilitatem addit sapiens. Utitur magni fluvii transitu. Hoc bonum.	First-six. (Represents) the extreme humility of the model man; is useful in wading through great streams, and is lucky.	The first line, divided, shows us the superior man who adds humility to humility. (Even) the great stream may be crossed with this, and there will be good fortune.

THE YH-KING AND ITS AUTHORS.

六二 鳴謙 貞吉	兼＝鶣 "the bird *Kien*." 0 0	(6th 2.) The singing bird *K'ien* (*Platalea major*.) 0 0	EPIPHONA SECUNDUM. Clamosa seu apparens humilitas, solidum bonum.	Second-six. (Represents) humility expressed, and brings good luck in completion.	The second line, divided, shows us humility that has made itself recognized. With firm correctness there will be good fortune.
九三 勞謙君子 有終吉	兼＝㑩 "along with." 兼＝挑 "satisfied."	(9th 3.) Labouring in accord with the princes, good issue. 0	EPIPHONA TERTIUM. Cum labore sapientis humilitas finera habet. Hoc bonum.	Third-nine. (Represents) the laborious and model humble man, is charged by the myriad of people.	The third line, undivided, shows the superior man of acknowledged merit. He will maintain his success to the end, and have good fortune.
六四 无不利 撝謙	兼＝嫌 "to dislike." 兼＝諫 "unassuming."	(6th 4.) Rejecting what does not suit. Unassuming.	EPIPHONA QUARTUM. Nihil est quod non conveniat. In omni motu est humilis.	Fourth-six. Is the exhibition of humility, and is in every way advantageous.	The fourth line, divided, shows one whose action would be in every way advantageous, stirring up (the more) his humility.

六五 不富以其鄰 利用侵伐 无不利	筮 = 賺 "underselling." 筮 = 賺 "to overcharge price." 筮 = 嫌 "to dislike."	(6–5.) Not rich by means of his neighbours. Many employ it in cheating and plundering. Rejecting what does not suit.	EPIPHONA QUINTUM. Cum non sit dives, utitur vicino. Oportet uti pugna et oppositione. Nihil est quod non conveniat.	Five-six. Is, employing the neighbours, although not rich; inflicting punishments is now profitable, and every advantage may now be obtained.	The fifth line, divided, shows one who, without being rich, is able to employ his neighbours. He may advantageously use the force of arms. All his movements will be advantageous.
上六 鳴謙利用行師征邑國	筮 = 鶼 "the *Kien* bird."	(Upper 6.) The singing bird *Platalea major* used to come by troops to the cities and states.	EPIPHONA SEXTUM. Clamosa humilitas. Utendo actione militari debet se opponere proprio regno.	Sixth-six. Is, the cry of humility; it is now advantageous to mobilize the army to subdue one's own state.	The sixth line, divided, shows us humility that has made itself recognized. The subject of it will with advantage put his hosts in motion; but (he will only) punish his own towns and states.

94. No observations are required on the following chapter, the xxxth, on 離 of which the primary orthograph was 閭 as we know by palæography. The author of the re-arrangement had not the same difficulties for the separation of the rows of characters into the seven lines, because of the great number of acceptations. He was obliged to put them up one after the other, not always separated by the word 若 or 如 "like." The same thing occurs several times in other chapters.[1]

In the last section of this paper we shall have to speak again of this chapter.

Here is the version:

---

[1] For instance, chapters iii., xxii., xxxv., etc.

78 THE YH-KING AND ITS AUTHORS.

95.—The XXXth Chapter 離, Anciently 囶 (A Vocabulary).

Text.	Our Version.		English.	Other Versions Compared.		
	Characters described.			P. Regis.	Rev. MacClatchie.	Dr. J. Legge.
	Old.	Modern.				
離利貞亨畜牝牛吉	囶 囶	離 離	*Li* has many exact significations. A domestic cow. 0	Li oportet ut sit solidum, ut sit penetrans. Si loctariam vaccam pascit, hoc bonum.	The Le diagram embraces benefit and luxuriance if moral rectitude is preserved; good luck now attends the rearing of cows.	Li indicates that, in regard to what it denotes, it will be advantageous to be firm and correct, and that thus there will be free course and success. Let (its subject) also nourish (a docility like that of) the cow, and there will be good fortune.
初九履	—	囶 = 摘 "to find shoes."	(First 9.) To shoe.	Epiphon. primum. Pedes inextricabiliter sunt impediti. Si observat, nullum est malum.	First-nine. (Represents) stepping out but not advancing, yet if caution is exercised no blame ensues.	The first line, undivided, shows one ready to move with confused steps. But he treads at the same time reverently, and there will be no mistake.
錯		囶 = 譎 "deceitful language."	Confused.			
然		囶 = 䄼 "to burn rice."	To burn.			
敬之无咎		囶 = 瞷 "to look at consecutively."	Attentive. 0 0			

THE YH-KING AND ITS AUTHORS.

六二 離 黃 離 元 吉	圉 = 離, 鶬 "the mango bird." —— —— "圉 = 圉 "brightness."	(6-2.) The yellow *Li* bird. 0 0	EPIPHON. SECUNDUM. Flava lux. Magnum bonum.	Second-six. Is yellow brightness and is supremely lucky.	The second line, divided, shows its subject in his place in yellow. There will be great good fortune.
九三 日 昃 之 離 不 鼓 缶 而 歌 則 大 耋 之 嗟 凶	圉 = 離 "to play on the *kin*." 圉 = 嗟 "perpetual chatter." —— ——	(9-3.) The shining of the declining sun. Is not to beat on an earthenware drum and sing (?) But is the fault of very old men. 0	EPIPHON. TERTIUM. Claritas solis deficit a meridie. Instrumentum sonorum non cantat; cum sit decrepitus suspirat, hoc pessimum.	Third nine. Is the light of the setting sun, when neither the beating of the earthenware drum nor singing (is heard); this is the sighing of old age and is unlucky.	The third line, undivided, shows its subject in a position like that of the declining sun. Instead of playing on his instrument of earthenware, and singing to it, he utters the groans of an old man of eighty. There will be evil.
九四 突 如 其 來 如 焚 如 死 如 棄 如	圉 = 圉 "to oppose." 圉 = 離 "to meet." 圉 = 烙 "a fire in a tent." 圉 = 離 "to depart from." 圉 = 離 "to dispense, to scatter."	(9-4.) Rushing against-like. His meeting one coming-like. Burning-like. Dying-like. Throwing off-like.	EPIPHON. QUARTUM. Veluti subito casu veniens, veluti comburens, veluti moriens, veluti deserens.	Fourth nine. Represents sudden approach or burning, or dying, or rejecting.	The fourth line, undivided, shows the manner of its subject's coming. How abrupt it is, as with fire, with death, to be rejected by all.

六五 出涕 沱若 戚嗟若 吉.	洵 = 滴 "diffusing by drops." 嗟 = 嚯 "to split wood."	(6–5.) "Coming out like falling tears." "As the sound of an axe." 0	EPIPHON. QUINTUM. Lacrimas ex oculis impetu decidunt. Tristis est velut singulibus anhelans. Hoc bonum.	Fifth-six. Is shedding tears like rain, sorrowing and sighing; but is lucky.	The fifth line, divided, shows its subject as one with tears flowing in torrents, and groaning in sorrow. There will be good fortune.
上六 王用出征 有嘉 折首 獲匪其醜 无咎	嘉 = 禧 "lucky omen." 僑 = 儔 "conjugal union." 離 = 雕 "to cut in two." 豸 = "a ravenous beast." 雊 = "a small basket." 籪 = "a sieve or winnowing basket." 區 = "a weird beast, a bogie."	(Upper 6.) The king uses it when going out to war. To have something happy especially a marriage. To cleave the head. A kind of wild beast. A square bamboo basket. A sieve or winnowing basket. Abominable, ugly. 0 0	EPIPHON. SEXTUM. Rex exeuntibus militibus utitur, est quid laude dignum. Praeclaros separat, illos socios non assumit, nullus est error.	Sixth-nine. Kings use (this stroke) when going out to subjugate their enemies; they obtain praise when the ringleaders are captured; if the entire gang is not seized, yet no blame arises.	The topmost line, undivided, shows the king employing its subject in his punitive expeditions. Achieving admirable (merit) he breaks (only) the chiefs (of the rebels). Where his prisoners were not their associates, he does not punish. There will be no error.

96. The following chapter translated, the thirty-first, on 咸, which is also a vocabulary, does not present so many meanings as the preceding, and it was not necessary to pile them up to the same extent. Besides, the meanings to be described were of peculiar difficulty in order to make the difference in the material and moral use of several of them intelligible. The meanings under i.–1, vi.–2, ix.–5, and upper 6, which are the various aspects of *one* same meaning, afford an interesting instance of the trouble taken by the original framers of the vocabulary to cope with the difficulty of making them clearly understood.

The character 咸, of which the ancient sound was *Kam* (or *Kom*), is a compound character which meant "to bite," and in its primary stage of symbolico-syllabism was written 咕 $\frac{m(\text{ou}}{\text{Ko-}}$ to be read from bottom to top.[1] *Kom* meaning "mouth hewing" *i.e.* "to bite" extended afterwards to the sense of "to seize, to shake, to move."

Ten foretelling words have to be dropped throughout the chapter.

---

[1] According to one of the laws of archaic orthography. *Vid.* § 23, note 2, p. 19.

97.—The XXXIst Chapter, on 咸 (A Vocabulary).

Text.	Our Version.			Other Versions Compared.		
	Characters described.		English.	P. Regis.	Rev. MacClatchie.	Dr. J. Legge.
	Old.	Modern.				
咸亨利貞取女吉	—	咸 = 咸 "union."	*Kien* means: 0 0 "to marry." 0	Kien est penetrans. Oportet ut sit soliditas. Si filiam uxorem ducat, hoc bonum.	Han implies luxuriance; benefit arises from the preservation of moral rectitude; to marry a wife is now lucky.	Hsien indicates that (on the fulfilment of the conditions implied in it) there will be free course and success. Its advantageousness will depend on the being firm and correct, (as) in marrying a young lady. There will be good fortune.
初六咸其拇	—	咸 = 咸 "to move."	(First-6.) "to move one's great toes."	Epiphon. primum. Pollicem digitum movet.	First-six. Is influencing the great toe (*i.e.* a slight first influence which afterwards pervades the whole mind.)	The first line, divided, shows one moving his great toes.

六二 咸 凶居	咸 = 拑 "to stir up." 咸 = 低 "uneasy."	(Six-two.) "to touch one's leg's calves." "Badly housed."	EPIPHON. SECUNDUM. Poplitis juncturam movet, hoc pessimum. Si stat hoc bonum.	Second-six. Is influencing the calf of the leg, and is unlucky; remaining stationary is lucky.	The second line, divided, shows one moving the calves of his leg. If he abide (quiet in his place) there will be good fortune.
九三 咸 執 其隨 往吝	咸 = 搖 "to shake." 咸 = 諧 "to harmonize."	(Nine-three.) 0 "to grasp." "one's yielding." "going with regret."	EPIPHON. TERTIUM. Coxendium movet et sequuntur quæ habet illi adhærentia, si eat pænitebit.	Third-nine. Is influencing the thigh, persistently following after the desires; in action shame results.	The third line, undivided, shows one moving his thighs and keeping close hold of those whom he follows. Going forward (in this way) will cause regret.
九四 貞吉亡 憧憧往來 朋從爾思	咸 = 誠 "lessening." 咸 = 撓 "to agitate." 咸 = 諧 "to sympathize."	(Nine-four.) 0 0 0 "Lost repentance." "wavering to and fro." "Friend following your thoughts."	EPIPHON. QUARTUM. Si solidum sit, bonum est. Nullus est pænitendi locus. Cum magna sollicitudine vadit et venit. Amici tuam mentum sequuntur.	Fourth Nine. Is lucky if moral rectitude be preserved, and then there exists no cause for regret; going backwards and forwards in an unsettled state friends are made according to the inclinations (i.e. not for their worth).	The fourth line, undivided, shows that firm correctness which will lead to good fortune, and prevent all occasions for repentance. If its subject be unsettled in his movements, (only) his friends will follow his purpose.

九五 咸其脢	咸 = 感 "to affect, to influence."	(Nine-five.) "moving internally."	EPIPHON. QUINTUM. Scapulas movet. Nullus est pænitendi locus.	Fifth-nine. Is influencing the back; no regret follows.	The fifth line, undivided, shows one moving the flesh along the spine above the heart. There will be no occasion for repentance.
无悔		○ ○			
上六 咸其輔頰舌	咸 = 齩 "to gnaw."	(Upper-six.) Moving one's jaws and tongue.	EPIPHON. SEXTUM. Mentum, genas et linguam movet.	Sixth six. Is influencing the jaws and tongue.	The sixth line, divided, shows one moving his jaws and tongue.

98. We hope that the preceding versions of four chapters will be considered as sufficient to exhibit the disposition of the chapters of the *Yh* made up of mere vocabularies. We shall now give an instance of a chapter in which has been embodied what we may call a ballad relating to an historical fact of the twenty-second century B.C., *viz.* the revolt of *Kwan*, the youngest son of the Emperor *K'i*, at the place of his exile (in modern Chih-li), where he had been sent most likely after intrigues which we may easily guess.

Here is the translation of this chapter, which treats on 觀, and which is the twentieth of the sixty-four chapters of the *Yh*.

86 THE YH-KING AND ITS AUTHORS.

99.—THE XXTH CHAPTER (VOCABULARY AND BALLAD).

TEXT.	OUR VERSION.			OTHER VERSIONS COMPARED.		
	CHARACTERS DESCRIBED.		ENGLISH.	P. REGIS.	REV. MACCLATCHIE.	DR. J. LEGGE.
	Old.	Modern.				
觀盥而不薦有孚顒若	雚 = 鸛 盥 = 盥 䙷 = 觀		KWAN (a small mug), to wash the hands before worship but not to offer;[1] to be depended on; as looking upwards.	Apponens non offert. Cum certa toneat rationi consonam personam exhibet.	The Kwan diagram implies having washed the hands, but not yet offered the sacrifice (*i.e.* looking up with expectation); the attitude is one of trustfulness and dignity.	Kwân shows (how ho whom he represents should be like) the worshipper who has washed his hands, but not (yet) presented his offerings; with sincerity and an appearance of dignity (commanding reverent regard).

[1] It was customary to wash the hands before offering sacrifice. According to the above text, the *Kwan* was used for that purpose, but not to make offerings, for which other kinds of vases were used.

THE YH-KING AND ITS AUTHORS.

Old Ballad.		Epiphon. primum.	First six.	
初六觀	(First-6.) The young Kwan (Son of the Emperor Ki).		(Represents) observing childishly; the inferior man (doing so) is blameless; but the model man (doing so) incurs shame.	The first line, divided, shows the looking of a lad;
小人无咎	The people did not blame (him).	Parvulus puer videt.		not blamable in men of inferior rank,
君子吝	The princes disliked (him).	Desipianti nulla est culpa; sapienti emolumentum.		but matter for regret in superior men.
六二闚觀	(6th 2.) Peeping at Kwan.	Epiphon. secundum. Videt extra eximis.	Second six. Is observing furtively, which tends to the preservation of chastity in females.	The second line, divided, shows one peeping out from a door. It would be advantageous if it were (merely) the firm correctness of a female.
利女貞	for many women was right.[1]	Convenit mulieri solidæ.		
六三觀我生進退	(6th 3.) Kwan, our begotten went (away) and returned.[1]	Epiphon. tertium. Vivendo vitam ingreditur et egreditur.	Third-six. Is observing my own life to regulate) advancing and receding.	The third line, divided, shows one looking at (the course of) his own life to advance or recede (accordingly).

[1] We have here a ballad relative to the youngest son of the Emperor K'i, 2197-2188 B.C. according to the chronology usually received and 1978-1957 according to the *Annals of the Bamboo Books*, where we find the following story which explains the above ballad: "In his eleventh year, the Emperor K'i banished his youngest son, the Martial Kwan 觀, beyond the Western Ho. In his fifteenth year the Martial Kwan with the people of the Western Ho rebelled. The Baron Show of Pang led a force to punish them, when the Martial Kwan returned to his allegiance." (*Cf.* Legge's *Chinese Classics*, vol. iii. p. 118.)

六四 觀國之光 利用賓于王	(6th 4.) Kwan's kingdom became glorious. Many as guests visited the king.	EPIPHON. QUARTUM. Videt gloriam regni. Erga regem debet haberi ut hospes.	Fourth-six. (Represents) observing the glory of the state; it is now profitable to act in an official capacity under the sovereign.	The fourth line, divided, shows one contemplating the glory of the kingdom. It will be advantageous for him, being such as he is (to seek) to be a guest of the king.
九五 觀我生 君子无咎	(9th 5.) Kwan, our begotten was a superior man. 0 0	EPIPHON. QUINTUM. Videt vitam nostram. Sapienti nulla est culpa.	Fifth-nine. Is observing one's own life; (in this) the model man is blameless.	The fifth line, undivided, shows its subject contemplating his own life (course). A superior man, he will (thus) fall into no error.
上六 觀其生 君子无咎	(Upper 6.) Kwan, he lived as a superior man. 0 0[1]	EPIPHON. SEXTUM. Videt vitam suam. Sapienti nulla est culpa.	Sixth-nine. Is observing the lives of others, (in which) the model man is blameless.	The sixth line, undivided, shows its subject contemplating his character to see if it be indeed that of a superior man. He will not fall into error.

[1] The two last characters are here, as in the preceding line, foretelling words and outside the rhymes.

100. The following and last chapter, of which space permits us to give the version in the present paper, is entirely ethnographical. It is the thirteenth in the series of the *Yh*, and it deals with the Troglodytes or Cave-men which formerly occupied several large regions in China previously to the Chinese conquest, and of whom sundry off-shoots still survive in rather out-of-the-way places inside and outside the Chinese dominion. When our complete translation is published, we shall give all the possible information on the subject in order to get the desired identification. The manners and customs of these tribes correspond precisely with those described in the *Yh*, and many of them have kept the same name, variously written 侗 洞 峒. Here is the translation:

101.—THE XIIITH CHAPTER, 同 人 *Tung jin* (ETHNOGRAPHICAL).

TEXT.	OUR VERSION.		OTHER VERSIONS COMPARED.		
	ENGLISH.		P. REGIS.	REV. MACCLATCHIE.	DR. J. LEGGE.
同人于野	The Troglodytes (which are) in the wild places.		Tong-jin id est Hominum conjunctio in deserto.	Tung jin extends (even) to rural regions, and implies luxuriantly abounding; wading through great streams is now profitable; and the model man gains advantage in the preservation of moral rectitude.	Thung Zăn (or Union of men) appears here (as we find it) in the (remote districts of the) country, indicating progress and success. It will be advantageous to cross the great stream. It will be advantageous to maintain the firm correctness of the superior man.
亨利涉大川	Many cross the river.		Est penetrato. Oportet transire magnum fluvium.		
利君子貞	Many (of them) are sages.		Oportet ut sit in soliditate sapientis.		

初九 同人于門 无咎	(First nine.) The Troglodytes come to (our) doors.　0　0	EPIPHON. PRIMUM. Esse ad januam simul cum homine, nullum est malum.	First nine. Represents associates at the gate (i.e. beginning a friendship); no blame ensues (the act being an unselfish one).	The first line, undivided, (shows the representatives of) the union of men just issuing from his gate. There will be no error.
六二 同人于宗 吝	(6–2.) The Troglodytes proceed to ancestral worship.	EPIPHON. SECUNDUM. Cum hominibus ad avos est pænitendi locus.	Second six. Is associating only with one's own clan; shame ensues (because it is a selfish proceeding).	The second line, divided, (shows the representative of) the union of men in relation with his kindred. There will be occasion for regret.
九三 伏戎于莽 升其高陵 三歲不興	(9–3.) Hiding their weapons in the bushes, they ascend to their high places, (and) during several years no more appear.	EPIPHON. TERTIUM. Miles in palude, est in insidiis; in monticulos ascendit; intra tres annos non assurget.	Third nine. Is planting an ambush in the jungle, and ascending a lofty mound (to reconnoitre); yet in three years (i.e. after a long time) the exploit is not accomplished.	The third line, undivided, (shows its subject) with his arms hidden in the thick grass, and at the top of a high mound. But for three years he makes no demonstration.

九四乘其吉墉弗克攻	(9–4.) Ascended to their forts they cannot be attacked. 0	Epiphon. Quartum. Supra ejus muros ascendentio non possunt pugnare. Hoc bonum.	Fourth nine. (Represents) ascending a city wall (to reconnoitre) because not being able to attack the enemy brings good luck, that is to say, (the soldiers) are wearied and return to their posts (without suffering defeat).	The fourth line, undivided, (shows its subject) mounted on the city wall; but he does not proceed to make the attack (he contemplates). There will be good fortune.
九五同人先號咷而後笑大師克相遇	(9–5.) The Troglodytes weep bitterly and then laugh. The grand teacher can understand them.	Epiphon. Quintum. Cum hominibus et jungens prius amare lacrymatur deinde ridet. Magnus exercitus post victoriam mutuo se adimunt.	Fifth nine. (Represents) weeping bitterly before associating in friendship, and afterwards rejoicing; also a great army which is able for the encounter.	In the fifth line, undivided, (the representative of the union of men first wails and cries out, and then laughs. His just host conquers, and he (and the subject of the second line) meet together.
上九同人于郊无悔	The Troglodytes proceed to sacrifices. 0 0	Epiphon. Sextum. Jungere se cum hominibus ad deserta. Nullus est poenitendi locus.	Sixth nine. (Represents) associating with friends in the suburbs; no regret ensues.	The topmost line, undivided, (shows the representative of) the union of men in the suburbs. There will be no occasion for repentance.

102. An interesting feature of this chapter is the remarkable proof it offers of the late addition of the foretelling words. The chapter is in verses, and the rhymes are easily recognized; 野 with 子·; 川 with 門; 宗 with 莽; 陵 with 與; 墉 with 攻; 眺 with 遇; 笑 with 郊. So that the foretelling words are no part of the ancient text, and have to be left aside ; they are : 亨, 貞, 无 咎, 吝, 吉, 无 悔. This is, I think, a very satisfactory demonstration.

X.—Contents Forgotten of the Yh.

103. In observing for our version of the *Yh-King* the principles of criticism laid down in the preceding section, we have been able to discover these remarkable facts,[1] that, in many chapters, the multifarious indications given by the characters in rows or isolated, are, within the chapter, just the various meanings more or less completely existing still and found in literature, of one ideographic character or expression represented more or less exactly by the modern heading of the same chapter.[2] These lists of values are occasionally accompanied by mythical, historical, geographical, ethnographical, ethical, astronomical, etc., references. Descriptions of aboriginal tribes of China; their customs, the meaning of some of their words, homonymous to the Chinese word which is the subject of the chapter, instructions to the officials about them, description of animals, birds, commercial and vulgar values, etc., are given as far as they exemplify the Chinese word.

104. The *Yh-King* has obviously been compiled of various old materials of different sorts and styles, which, misunderstood, have been arranged, classified, divided in lines, corrected and completed by the addition of many of the foretelling words which have been interspersed in the text.[3] Short sentences and rows of characters have been, with the help of the changes of writing, strained into meanings supposed to have been

---

[1] *Vid.* my *Early History of the Chinese Civilization*, p. 25.
[2] Excepting the alterations voluntarily introduced since.
[3] *Vid.* above, § 13.

expressed by Wen Wang, the presumed editor of the book, and related to the immediate period previous to him, but with which they had originally no connection whatever. An interesting feature is, to be able to detect how, from independent rows of characters, not intended for the purpose, the correspondence which seems to exist between the contents of the chapters and the six whole and broken groups composing the sixty-four hexagrams or Kwas of the same number of chapters was obtained. A brief examination of the whole easily explains the process by which the regular classification and division into the desired number of 64 chapters of 7 lines has been got up. In the case of words having an insufficient number of meanings to fill up the required seven lines, the same meaning is repeated sometimes variously, as often as necessary; in reverse cases, the meanings have been strung together one after the other like a thread of beads; and as the subject-matters were not of the required number of 64, several have been cut in two, and a few more modern texts have been added.

105. The *Yh-King* seems to have been arranged at first under the Hia dynasty (2205–1766 B.C.); and when it reached the hands of Wen Wang, it was already used for divination. Its broken and numerous meanings progressively misunderstood by the changes occurring in the language, the growth of the dialects and the discrepancies introduced in the writing by oblivion of the old rules of orthography, had made of these ancient documents a very suitable reference to pick up prognostics. The text had been connected with the 64 Kwas, and every chapter divided most likely into two parts, in order to correspond to the two trigrams of each hexagram. Wen Wang in 1143 B.C. subdivided the text and modified it as we have seen, he added as an explanation of his rearrangement the first wing beginning with 彖 曰 *Twan says*, and his son Chöu Kung added in turn, the second wing beginning with 象 曰 *Siang says*, in the ordinary editions of the *Yh*.

106. To resume the question, the text of the *Yh-King* is nothing else than a general vocabulary of a small number

(about 60) of words and expressions. And, no doubt, the impossibility of reading as current phrases and text, simple lists of meanings [as if we should try to read Johnson's Dictionary as we would read a novel], accounts for the absolute obscurity of the book and the astounding number of interpretations which have been proposed by native Chinese scholars, a path in which they have been uselessly followed by several European Sinologists.

107. The *Yh-King* is not the only book whose fate has been to be misunderstood. Many of the Vedic hymns have had their primary object and views entirely turned away. In Japan, too, we have a very striking example, to which we shall refer presently. But the *Yh-King* is the only one which, having to be transcribed several times through successive changes of writing and the improvement of characters in order to precise their sense, has been exposed to all the consequences of the process and has accordingly suffered.

108. The Japanese example is sufficiently striking to be placed side by side with the protracted misunderstanding of the *Yh-King*, though not with the gradual and eventual transformation of the text of the Chinese mysterious book. The *Nihongi* has met the same fate of a forced interpretation, which afterwards was recognized as the result of an improper intelligence of the style in which it was originally written. The *Yamatobumi* 日本書記 or *Nippon-syo-ki*[1] (vulg. *Nihongi*), containing the oldest history of Japan, from 661 B.C. till 696 A.D., was published in 720 A.D. as manuscript in thirty parts. It was worded in Chinese and written in Hing-shu 行書 or running hand Chinese characters.[2] At that time Chinese composition was extensively used in Japan, but afterwards since the period Yengi (A.D. 901) intercourse with China ceased and no more students went to that country, so that finally a peculiar Japanese style of Chinese composition arose, in which the characters were not read

---

[1] These two readings illustrate the two modes of reading the Chinese characters in Japan, according to their sound (*Koye*) or to their meaning (*Yomi*). *Cf.* J. J. Hoffmann, *A Japanese Grammar* (Leiden, 1868, 8vo.), p. 4.

[2] Hoffmann, *Japanese Grammar*, p. 5.

in the same order as they were written. Those coming
first in order when writing a sentence being placed at the
end of the sentence in reading ; the characters forming no
complete meaning if read as they were written. This hybrid
style is in use at the present time for epistolary correspondence
and for government documents.[1] In order to avoid any
misunderstanding, in modern texts special small signs are
placed on the lower left hand side of the Chinese characters
to indicate the transposition required. The *Nihongi,* as other
books of the same time, being written in Chinese, " the
unlettered could not understand it without explanation.
Hence there existed in the middle ages rules for the interpretation of this history, and gradually it came to be considered as a religious work on Shintoism. Both Shinto and
Buddhist priests explained it as a work on Confucianism or
Buddhism, so that at last incorrect opinions and statements
were formed, with which the ignorant were misled. Owing
to the frequent wars, however, these doctrines were neglected,
and at last there were none who believed in them."[2] Even-
tually, eight hundred years after (since A.D. 1688–1703), the
erroneous opinions of the scholars of the middle ages were
corrected, and the proper reading of the ancient texts was
recovered.

109. What happened to the illustrious German philosopher
Schöpenhauer, with the first imperfect and misleading version
of the Upanishads,[3] might be quoted as another instance of

---

[1] Vid. *An Outline History of Japanese Education, Literature and Arts*; prepared by the Mamkusho (Department of Education), Tokio, Japan, 1877, 12mo.
p. 145.

[2] *Outline History of Japanese Education,* p. 146.

[3] The first version of the Upanishads made into any European language was by
the famous traveller Anquetil Duperron, from the Persian ; he seems to have
made both a French and Latin translation, the latter alone having been published
(A.D. 1801–1802). It was written in a style utterly unintelligible except to the
most lynx-eyed of philosophers. Amongst these, the celebrated Schöpenhauer
distinguished himself by his open avowal: "In the whole world there is no study,
except that of the originals, so beneficial and so elevating as that of the ' Oupnek-
hat.' It has been the solace of my life, it will be the solace of my death." It is
difficult to understand how the translation of Duperron could provide this double
solace. The opening words of his translation are these: "*Oum* hoc verbum (esse)
adkit ut sciveris, sic Jò *maschgouli* fac (de eo meditare) quod ipsum hoc verbum
aodkit est; propter illud quod hoc (verbum) *oum*, in Sam Beïd, cum voce altâ,
cum harmoniâ pronunciatum fiat."—Vol. i. p. 15.

an important work misunderstood, and nevertheless satisfying somehow minds fond of nebulous statements in which their imagination could freely exercise itself.

XI.—Origin of the Yh-King.

110. Proofs of various kinds: similitude of institutions, traditions and knowledge, affinities of words of culture; and in what concerns the writing: likenesses of shapes of characters, hieroglyphic and arbitrary, with the same sounds (sometimes polyphons) and meanings attached to them, the same morphology of written words, the same phonetic laws of orthography, had led me, several years ago,[1] to no other conclusion than that (as the reverse is proved impossible by numerous reasons), at an early period of their history and before their emigration to the far East, the Chinese *Bak* families had borrowed the pre-cuneiform writing and elements of their knowledge and institutions from a region connected with the old focus of culture of South-Western Asia.[2]

The similarities in shapes, sounds, and meanings of characters[3] show that the borrowing was done at the period when the Cuneiform strokes already introduced were not yet exclusively used to draw the characters, straight and curved lines being still used at the same time, and the introduction of the wedge-shaped implement had not effaced the pictographical forms of the signs.[4]

---

[1] *Vid.* the bibliographical information in § i. n. 1 of the present paper.

[2] The late period of the extension is shown by the state of oblivion in which the early Chinese Bak families were, in regard to the primitive meaning of many characters, their mistakes on that subject, and the many later notions from Babylonian arts and knowledge which they had borrowed at the same time. The peculiarities of the connexion of the archaic Chinese characters and the Babylonian writing, for instance, in the case of the cardinal points, show unmistakably that the borrowing was not made before the Semitic influence took the lead over the Akkado-Sumerian sway.

[3] When I pointed out in May, 1880 (*Early History*, p. 29), the shifting of the points of the compass, I did not hope that this statement would so soon receive a brilliant confirmation, from the Assyrian side. Cf. the decipherment of a tablet secured by the British Museum, July 27th, 1881, by Mr. T. G. Pinches, *Proceedings of the Society of Biblical Archæology*, Feb. 6th, 1883. The great importance of the fact is that it gives a hint on the date of the extension of the writing from S.W. Asia to China, and a clue to the Zodiacal difficulty which Dr. G. Schlegel has tried to solve in adding 17000 years, which are now unnecessary.

[4] This is shown not only by some early Chinese characters containing such strokes, but also by various traditions speaking of strokes broad at one end and

111. A most interesting feature of the literature embodied in the cuneiform characters is the numerous vocabularies (known wrongly as syllabaries) framed for the understanding of the characters and texts of antiquity. They may be roughly divided into two classes, being vocabularies of several kinds giving the different meanings, various sounds, Sumerian, Akkadian, Assyrian, and the Akkadian descriptive names of the characters, single and compound. One class gives the meanings and sounds of one character; the other class the various characters of one meaning, or of objects of the same kind. They are phonetic and ideologic vocabularies, as, for example, in Chinese, the Yh-King's phonetic vocabularies, and the old dictionary Œĭ-ya's ideological lists.

Without exception the so-called Cuneiform syllabaries hitherto found and deciphered are only copies made by order of the Assyrian or Babylonian monarchs. That the originals of these copies were the primitive ones is very dubious. There are reasons and even facts which tend to show that the process of framing lists of those classes is nearly as old as the systematization of the writing in horizontal lines, or has been required, if not by the reform, at least by the ethnological extension of the pre-Cuneiform script and writings.

114. Admitting by the force of overwhelming evidence, the borrowing by the Chinese Bak families of the script and elements of culture from this lexico-making people, we have to recognize the probability of their borrowing at the same time, as was unavoidable, some of these vocabularies. The remarkable similarity of shape, polyphony and various meanings between some of these cuneiform phonetic lists appended to one character, and some of the Yh-King's chapters, as for example between those represented by 臣 and 鬲, 彔 and 貴, 臣 and 艮, ch. 30, 22, 52, would suggest that some of the *Yh-King's* vocabularies are imitated form old pre-Cuneiform ones.

115. Let us take, for instance, the character 臣 *lu* "a

---

pointed at the other. We have, however, to take into account the change in appearance of the characters, caused by the use of another material than the clay tablets and of another tool than the triangular-shaped one used for the impression of the cuneiform strokes.

bull,"[1] of which the oldest shape is the same as the archaic form of 畧 *li* "a cow." The various acceptations of the Cuneiform character *lu* in the syllabaries, and those of the Chinese character *li*, indicated in the XXXth chapter of the *Yh*, a chapter of which it is the subject-matter, ought to correspond, if we are right in our statements. The ancient sounds of the Chinese word were *lip, dep, de*;[2] those of the wedge-written character were *lup, dip, udu*.[3] On the so-called syllabary-tablets, the character 𒂍 single or reduplicated has the following acceptations:

	𒂍	*immerŭ*	= "lamb."
	𒂍	*gŭkkallum*	= "sheep" (?).
	𒂍	*ṣabatum*	= "to seize."
𒂍	𒂍	*śimdilu*	= "a bucket."
𒂍	𒂍	*tintum*	= "law, order."
𒂍	𒂍	*sitmanu*	= "keeping."
𒂍	𒂍	*ritbusu*	= "lying down."
𒂍	𒂍	*silpuru*	= "sending."
𒂍	𒂍	*kurrumu*	= "encircling."[4]

Unfortunately a great many values of the sign are lost in consequence of the fractures of the tablets, the principal fracture leaves a lacuna of six or eight lines[5] lost, representing at least as many words. On the other hand, the decipherment of historical inscriptions has revealed several of these lost mean-

[1] In the bilingual list (*Cuneiform Inscriptions of Western Asia*, vol. ii. p. 44) *lu* is found (as borrowed from the Akkadian stock) with Assyrian complements precising the gender and number, viz.: *lû* (a bull), *lûlû* (a cow), *lunim* (oxen). *Lû* is the word as borrowed from the Akkadian; *lûlû* is the word with the Assyrian feminine ending; *lûnim* is the plural masculine, explaining the foregoing groups. The entry succeeds another meaning "oxen." Mr. T. G. Pinches has found this and other information quoted below, on my pointing out to him, by the help of the Chinese, that the characters ought to have the meaning of "a bull" or "a cow," hitherto unknown by the Assyriologists.
[2] Decayed into *Li* and *che*. The final *p* has been lost very early, but traces of it are still found, and the restoration is perfectly justified by many cases. *Cf.* for instance: Min tsi ki, *Luh shu tung*, K. i. f. 22 *v*. *Vid.* also J. Edkins, *Introduction to the Study of Chinese Characters*, p. 108, number 724.
[3] A syllabary in four columns of the Sp. II. collection in the British Museum, gives as the name of this sign *lu* the word (*lu-up*=) *lup*, thus indicating the full form of the word.—T. G. Pinches, *MS. note*.
[4] *Vid. Cuneiform Inscriptions of Western Asia*, vol. iii. p. 70 lines 58, 59, 60; vol. ii. p. 22. Fred. Delitzsch, *Assyrische Lesestücke*, pp. 36, 58, 25; and also T. G. Pinches, *MS. note*.
[5] *Vid. Cun. Insc. W. A.*, vol. iii. pp. 69-70. F. Delitzsch, *Assyr. Les.* p. 65.

ings, such as "to approach, to burn, to cross, to spoil, to hold," etc.[1]

116. Now let us remember that these acceptations of the Cuneiform character, in the above case as in others, were written some thousands of years ago, and since that time have no more been exposed to the fluctuations which constantly occur in word-meanings. They have been buried under the ruins of the civilization which produced them, and their language is dead for eighty generations. On the Chinese side no burial nor death has taken place; some kind of crystallization has produced itself in the mind of the middle-kingdom-man by his exaggerated veneration for anything which he has received or assumes that he has received from his ancestors; and though the ground-work of the syllabaries, like chapters included by ignorance in the Yh-King, is undoubtedly a very early compilation, it must not be forgotten that they have been transcribed again and again, re-written and re-arranged by Wen Wang, and, besides that, exposed to all the alterations and transformations of a writing and a language still living.

With all these *impedimenta* in the way of comparison, and all these causes of divergence, are not the parallelism and resemblances of meanings something wonderful? After having referred to the various acceptations of the character 閑, as indicated in the chapter relating to it, given above (§ 95), it is impossible not to be struck by the evidence that the two systems and the two texts are related one to the other. It would be rather a bold conclusion to say that they are the same lists; the Chinese being the copy of the other, with no other discrepancies than those of time, space and language; but what is pretty sure is, that the Chinese vocabularies have been framed in obedience to the same principles, with the same materials, and undoubtedly according to the tradition of the old syllabaries of South-Western Asia.

117. The same principles having been traditional on the two

---

[1] *Cf.* with caution, Rev. A. Sayce, *Assyrian Grammar*, and E. de Chossat, *Repertoire Assyrien*, s.v., because of the progress of decipherment since the publication of their works.

sides, it is no more a remarkable fact, though a convincing evidence, to find in the two countries, besides the phonetic vocabularies, the converse system, *i.e.* lists of the words or characters having a common meaning. The old Chinese dictionary, the 爾雅 *Œl-ya*, is nothing else than an ideological vocabulary. If we take, in the first part (釋詁 *Shih Ku*, which is said to have been arranged from old documents by Chöu Kung in the twelfth century B.C.), the list of the words for *king* or *prince*, and restore their older forms in order to read their old sounds, and then compare it with a list of the same kind published in pl. 30, i. of the *Cuneiform Inscriptions of Western Asia*, vol. v., we cannot help seeing many words common in the two lists, showing that these lists have been drawn from materials differentiated from one same stock.

118. It would certainly be unwise, though not hopeless, the historical and geographical distances having been extended as they have, to expect the discovery of the same texts in Chinese and in Cuneiform. In the lapse of time which has occurred since the communication of culture and probably of written documents, these have varied. They have been transcribed, according to the changes of the writing, or, what is much more probable, they have been lost on the Chinese side, which had to keep them twenty-five centuries more to hand them to us. A few fragments may however have survived among a people so fond of tradition as the Chinese are. This would be the explanation of the extraordinary similitude of some of the Yh-King lists with some Cuneiform lists.

119. As a matter of probability, it seems only natural that the early leaders of the Chinese Bak families, instructed by the culture of South-Western Asia, should have been induced not only to keep some lists of the values of the written characters they had learned and wanted to transmit, but also to continue the same practice of making lists relating to the peoples, customs, etc., of their new country.

As a matter of fact the *Yh-King* is the oldest of the Chinese

---

[1] *Vid.* above § 23 n.

books, not certainly as it now stands, but as far as concerns the greatest part of the documents which are compiled in it. Some of these parts are most likely contemporary with the early leaders of the Chinese Bak families (*Pöh Sing*). It has all the appearance of being a series of notes, documents, and informations collected by the early chiefs of the Chinese immigrants. It looks like a repository of indications drawn up by the early leaders of the Bak families, for the guidance of their officers and successors, in the use of the characters of the writing, by the native populations with whom the newly arrived people had to deal, for the customs, the produce of the soil, the animal kingdom, etc.; and it is, in this sense, that the *Yh-King* is the most valuable of the Chinese classics, the one in which, according to the non-interrupted and unconscious feeling of the Chinese themselves, was embodied the wisdom and knowledge of the sages of yore.

It has been deeply modified and somewhat augmented in the course of time, and with the extensive emendations made to the text, the possibility of finding out the primitive meanings can hardly be expected in every case; the contrary would be surprising with so many difficulties to overcome. Be that as it may, the remarkable results of these researches make the *Yh-King* a much higher and more useful book than it had previously been supposed to be. It is not a mysterious book of fate and prognostics. It contains a valuable collection of documents of old antiquity in which is embodied much information on the ethnography, customs, language and writing of early China.

XII.—Material History of the Yh-King.

118. The primitive texts of the *Yh* were necessarily written in *Ku-wen* style of characters, and as usual engraved[1] on wood or bamboo tablets. It was during the eventful period of that

---

[1] Not scratched, but cut incuse with a graving knife, in characters thick at one end and thin at the other. *Cf.* T. de L., *The old Babylonian characters and their Chinese derivates*, § 23.—The famous inscription of the Great Yü, always quoted as an instance of early Chinese characters, cannot be older than the fifth century B.C., while the sinuosities and irregularities of the strokes have been only the result of the abrasion of the stone.

style of writing that the work was re-arranged, and that the most numerous substitutions, additions and suppressions of characters took place. It does not appear that the *Yh* was transcribed in the *Ta chuen*, or great curved characters of 820, but without preventing its preservation in the oldest style, it was re-written for practical use as a book of devination, in the *chuen* or *curved* characters (mixed of *Ku-wen* and *ta chuen* principles) which was current between the end of the eighth and the first quarter of the third century B.C. The process was then to write with a bamboo calamus dipped in lacquer on slips of bamboo, and the *Ku-wen* text was also copied in that way.

119. In 227 B.C. appeared the *Siao chuen* or lesser curved character, which was simply an official adoption, and partial completion, of the system of simplifying the written characters, a habit which had gradually come into practice for two centuries. Fifteen years afterwards, the *Li shu*, a square, bold and thick mode of writing with the brush, newly invented, came into use for administrative purposes. The year before, *i.e.* in 213 B.C., had begun the celebrated persecution of the Hwang-Ti, the first Emperor of China, against the traditional literature of antiquity; but it did not affect the fate of the *Yh*, which was amongst the works excepted by special order. The work transcribed in the *chuen* was also written in the *Li shu* styles, with a new confirmation of many supposed meanings by new substitutions of characters, and the changes or additions of determinatives which had come into greater use during and since the *chuen* period.[1] It was then written with the hair-pencil on rolls of silk-cloth.

120. The great trouble, which gave to the literati during the Renaissance of literature the recovery of many works hidden in out-of-the-way places during the persecution, and the loss of many others, led them to invent a new mode of preserving the sacred books, and at the same time avoid any corruptions of the text. Paper came into current use at the beginning of the second century, but it does not seem to have

---

[1] *Cf. suprà* p. 22, and *Catalogue of Chinese Coins*, p. xxxv.-xxxvi.

had any influence on the preservation of the *Yh*, or any other of the classics, because the former systems were not discarded for some time, and the ancient copies had not disappeared. The lacquered tablets of the classics which had been discovered in 154 B.C., hidden in the ancient house of Confucius, were preserved in the Royal Archives, where those which had escaped the bibliothecal catastrophes of the years 23 and 290 remained until 311 A.D., when they were lost in the great fire which destroyed the precious library once collected by the Wei dynasty.

121. The year 175 A.D. saw put in practice the grandest idea of the time, in view of securing evermore the integrity of the sacred books. Tsai-yung, duly authorised by the Emperor HAN-LING-TI, after a careful revision of the text of six kings,[1] by competent scholars, wrote them himself in red on 46 stela. The engraving and erection of the tablets was finished in 183 A.D., in front of the Imperial College, on the east side at Loh-yang. Their text was threefold, *Ku-wen*, *Chuen* and *Li shu*.[2] Students were allowed to take rubbings of the stones, and the result was that less than a century afterwards five of the stela had disappeared, only twelve were still intact, and twenty-nine were either broken or defaced. Those which had contained the *Yh-King* were no longer recognisable.[3] In order to obviate the gradual disparition which was going on in their time, the Emperors of Wei had taken some important measures. In the years 240–248 A.D., the ruling prince, Tsi Wang Tang, had the *Shu-King* engraved again, and also the *Tchun tsiu* with the *Tso tchuen*, on both sides of 48 stelas in the same three styles of characters. The *Ku-wen* part was engraved after the tracings taken in 220 A.D. by Tch'un from the wooden tablets of the Royal Archives.

122. Subsequently and before the end of their dynasty in 265, the Wei had also the text of the *Yh-King, Shu-King,*

---

[1] Not five kings, as sometimes repeated.
[2] Cf. *Hou Han shu:* Tsai yung biography.
[3] Cf. the statements of Luh Ki, in his *Loh yang Ki*. He lived 260-303 A.D. He could recognize only parts of the *Shu King, Kung-yang's* commentary with the Chun Tsiu, *Lun-yu Li-Ki*, and nothing from the *Yh* and *Shi* Kings.

Kung-yang, and *Li Ki* in the Li shu characters engraved on both sides of 48 other stone tablets, as a pendant to the other set.

123. These remarkable monuments did not remain intact. In the middle of the fifth century, out of an original number of 144, only 91 remained, viz. 18 of the Han period, 25 of the treble-styled ones of 248, and all the 48 in *Li shu*. These 91 dwindled down to 52 in 550, and to 50 in 600 A.D. At the latter date only five of the tablets of Tsai yung were still in existence. In 717 the 48 tablets of 248 were reduced to 13. Several removals in 546, 580 and 586 had taken place to their greatest injury. All that remains of them since that time is preserved at Si-ngan fu, in the famous *Pei-lin* or Forest of Tablets, amongst the three hundred inscriptions which it contains.

124. In the winter quarter of 717, an Imperial proclamation was issued that search should be made for lost writings. A commission of 23 scholars was appointed to this effect; they laboured for nine years editing and printing texts, and then presented to the throne a copy of their work in 48,000 sections.[1] Ancient texts had been printed before, notably in 593 B.C., but the sacred books themselves were not included in one or the other of these two occasions. Their texts, however, could but be directly or indirectly preserved by the new art, either by direct printing under private enterprise or by the imperial editions of some of the commentaries upon them. It was only in 932 that an imperial order was issued to engrave on wood and print for distribution the nine kings recognized at the time. The work was finished in 952, and was made according to the current text.[2]

125. Some of the ancient texts were also preserved by printing. We have mentioned p. 40, the *Ku wen* text of the *Yh-King*, of which an edition printed in 1596 was once in the library of Pauthier. Unhappily we have not yet been

---

[1] Cf. *Kang kien ta tsuen*, R. 38, f. 16.—L. C. Hopkins, *The Six scripts*, p. 36.—Also *Kang kien tcheng she-ti*, K. 23, f. 10.
[2] Cf. *King y k'ao*, R. 293, f. 1 sq.; *T'ung kien kang muh*, K. 56, f. 22v., R. 59, f. 10; *Li tai ki sze*, R. 80, f. 13, 17; G. Pauthier, *Mémoires* ii. *l.c.* p. 414-416.

able to consult a copy of the same, and we urge our colleagues in Sinology to help us in the matter.

In 1049–1054, a scholar named Su-wang discovered some original rubbings which had been taken on the three character stone classics of the Wei dynasty, *i.e.* the 48 tablets erected in 240–248 A.D., and he had them engraved and published at Loh-yang. In 1806 Sun-ting-yen republished them after a copy of Su-wang's work, which had come into his hands. It includes 307 characters *Ku-wen*, 217 *Chuen* and 295 *Li shu*, of the *Shu King*, *Chun tsiu* and *Tso tchuen*.[1]

Some editions of the chuen text of the classics have been published by Imperial order. The latest is entitled *Kin ting chuen wen luh king sze shu*, i.e. the chuen text of the six kings and four canonical books edited by Imperial commission.

126. In 744, Hiuen Tsung of the T'ang dynasty, appointed a commission of scholars, under the presidency of Wei Pao, to substitute for the *Li shu* characters the form which was current in his day.[2] That was the *Heng-shu* or current hand which, initiated by Liu Teh-cheng in 165 A.D. had been improved by Wang Hien-chi, who died in 379 A.D. This event is told at the occasion of the *Shu king*.[3] Nothing precisely is said of a similar change at that time for the other classics; but it seems extremely probable that the work was accomplished by the same commission.

127. In the following century a new set of stone classics was erected at Chang-ngan (Si-ngan fu). Five years (833–837) were spent to engrave the twelve works they included on 216 tablets. The *Yh-King* occupied the first nine.[4] They are still at present, hardly injured, in the "Forest of Tablets" at Si-ngan fu,[5] which we have already mentioned, and where they continue to be the gaze of a host of students.

---

[1] *Cf.* Sun Sing yen, *Wei san li shih king wei tze k'ao*.—A copy of this precious little work exists in the British Museum.
[2] The National Library of Paris has an edition (without title-page) in the Chuen character of the *Yh, Shu, Shi, Chun-tsiu, Y-li* and *Chōu-li*.
[3] *Tze hioh tien*, K. i. f. 22 *v*.
[4] Wang Chang, *Kin shih tsui pien*, R. 109.—*Li tai ki sze*, K. 70, f. 22 *v*.— G. Pauthier, O.C., p. 405-406.
[5] *Cf.* A. Williamson, *Journeys in North China*, 1870, vol. i. p. 380.

The characters are in the *heng shu* style, and present but very few and unimportant discrepancies with those of modern time.

Although it had been customary under former dynasties to remove with them the stone libraries at every transfer of capital, the stone classics have remained in the town where they had been erected. But the northern capital, under the present dynasty, could not remain without similar monuments. During the reign of Kien lung, 182 stone tablets engraved on both sides,[1] containing the thirteen classics, executed in a style of great beauty, were erected at Peking, and are admired to the present day in the old *Kwoh tze kien*.

Such have been the material circumstances concerning the preservation of the *Yh King*.

Concluding Chapter.—The Yh-King and the Western Origin of the Chinese Civilisation.

I.

128. The language of the Bak families, which under the leadership of *Yu Nai Hwang-ti* (Hu Nak-Kunte)[2] arrived about 2282 B.C. on the banks of the Loh river in Shensi,[3] was deeply connected with that of the Akkado-Sumerians of Elam-Babylonia. This alone might be sufficient to show that previously to their migration to the East and the Flowery Land they were settled in the vicinity—probably in the North East—of these populations, and therefore in

---

[1] *Cf.* W. A. P. Martin, *The Kwoh tze Kien*, an old Chinese University: —The *Chinese Recorder*, 1871, p. 86.

[2] On this identification Cf. my monograph on *The Onomastic similarity of Nai Hwang-ti of China and Nakhunte of Susiana*, London, 1890, 10 pp.; and B. and O. R., vol. iv. pp. 256-264.

[3] The first year of Yu-Nai Hwang-ti, independently of the miscalculated astronomical recurrences which have perverted the Ancient Chinese chronology variously arranged by native scholars from the Han to the Sung dynasties, has been found on purely traditional grounds, by Hwang P'u-mi, a great scholar of A. D. 215-282, in his works *Ti wang she ki* and *Nien lih*, to have happened in a year which corresponds to our 2332 B.C. And the annals of the Bamkoo Books (*Tchuh shu ki nien* I., i., 3) state as the first geographical entry that Hwang-ti, in the 50th year of his reign, sacrificed near the Loh river (in Shensi S.E.).

proximity of the Chaldean civilisation, with which we have shown them to have been so well acquainted.[1] The relationship of their language with that of the Akkado-Sumerians was pointed out and exemplified by me in 1880, and repeatedly since then in subsequent publications. I thought at first that the connection was such that comparative philologists might be compelled to include the ancient Chinese and the Akkado-Sumerian dialects in one and the same group of the Ural-Altaic languages.[2] But a more extensive comparison has shown me that the Akkado-Sumerian words in Chinese belong to three successive strata: (1) Words belonging to the common inheritance of the two languages from the original Turano-Scythian linguistic stock to which they belonged and from which they have separately and greatly diverged, through their contact with other languages;[3] (2) Words of culture received by the Bak families from the Elamo-Babylonian civilisation in which they were current terms;[4] (3) Words which have entered China through intermediate and later channels.

129. At present the Turano-Scythian stock of languages is divided into six principal groups:—

1. *S. W. Asiatic*: Akkado-Sumerian, etc.
2. *Uralic*: Ugro-Finnish; Samoyed; Tungusic; Japanese.
3. *Altaic*: Turkish; Mongol.
4. *Küenlunic*: Kotte; Chinese; Tibeto-Burmese.
5. *Himalaic*: Dravidian; Gangetic; Kolarian; etc.
6. *Caucasic*: N. Caucasian; Alarodian.[5]

---

[1] In numerous publications referred to in the following notes.

[2] *Early history of the Chinese Civilisation*, 1880, pp. 19-21, where I gave a comparison of fifty words identical in the two languages.

[3] This is shown by the successive changes which have occurred in their respective ideologies. The ideological indices of the Chinese were at first iii. 1, 3, 5, 8; passing through iv. 1, 3, 6, 7, and vi. 2, 3, 6, 8, they are now settled at vi. 1, 3, 6, 8.—Those of the Akkado-Sumerian from iii. 1, 3, 5, 8, have passed to i. 1, 3, 5, 8, and iii. 2, 4, 5, 8. The standard indices of the Turano-Scythian stock are iii. 1, 3, 5, 8.

[4] *Cf.* my work on the *Origin of the early Chinese civilisation from Babylonia, Elam, and later western sources*, ch. iv. note 54; B. and O. R. 1889, vol. iii. p. 77.

[5] The Euskarian is perhaps the sole representative diverged and altered of a seventh group.

The arrangement[1] may not, and probably does not, correspond to the original sub-division, as the geographical locations were different from what they are at present; but a deep relationship older than their division and multiplication in groups exists between these languages, and as this relationship is a result of common descent from an original nucleus of dialects neighbouring one another, the older the language of a group, the greater must be its affinity with any other old language of a different group. Hence the comparisons which have been established on equally good grounds between the Akkado-Sumerian and the Uralic languages by François Lenormant,[2] the Altaic languages by Prof. Fritz Hommel,[3] and the Chinese languages by myself, and lately and more fully by the Rev. C. J. Ball.[4] Similar comparisons between Akkado-Sumerian, Tibeto-Burmese, and Dravidian languages would prove equally successful. But the reasons previously stated make the relationship with the ancient Chinese particularly extensive without it be necessary to assume, as an explanation of the case, that the Chinese language is a modern representative of the Ancient Akkadian.

---

[1] On these groups *cf.* the standard works of Dr. Heinrich Wenkler, *Uralaltaische Völker und Sprachen*, Berlin, 1884; *Das Uralaltaische und seine Gruppen*, Berlin, 1885. Also T. de L., *The Languages of China before the Chinese* (Presidential Address to the Philological Society, 1886); second edition enlarged, in French, 1888, 210 pp.. Alfred Maury, *Journal des Savants*, 1889, Oct. 473-485, Sept. 577-566. R. de la Grasseerie, *Des recherches récentes de la linguistique relatives aux langues de l'Extrême Orient, principalement d'après les travaux de M. Terrien de Lacouperie*. Paris, Imprimerie Nationale, 1891, 31 pp.

[2] *La langue Primitive de la Chaldée et les idiômes Touraniens*, Paris, 1875; *Chaldæan Magic*, London, 1877, 144 pp.

[3] *Die Sumero-Akkadische Sprache und ihre Verwandtschaftverhaltnisse*, pp. 65 (Zeitschrift für Keilschriftforschung), Munich, 1884; *The Sumerian language and its affinities*, 13 pp. J.R.A.S. 1886, vol. xviii. T. de L., *Akkadian and Sumerian in Comparative Philology*, 7 pp., *The Babylonian and Oriental Record*, Nov. 1886, vol. i.

[4] T. de L., *Early history of the Chinese Civilisation*, pp. 19-21. Also C. J. Ball, *The New Accadian*, 122 pp. (P.B.A., 1889-1890), who has omitted to acknowledge that I had been the first to open the field. The author, in order to avoid to some extent the many pitfalls inherent to comparison of monosyllables, has ingeniously proceeded by groups in his assimilations, and has thus undoubtedly proved a deep relationship between the vocabulary of the two languages, although about one-third of his Chinese words are misconceived or not old.

II.

131. It is not unimportant that this distinction should be clearly understood, as otherwise an easy confusion might arise in the minds of our readers and lead them to expect between the Akkado-Sumerians of Babylonia and the ancient civilizers of China, a continuity and parallelism of descent and tradition, which is contrary to the historical evidence collected some years since in long and extensive researches. The Akkado-Sumarians were not the civilizers of Chaldæo-Babylonia. They were still rude and in a primitive stage of social development when they came down from the mountains of the north-east to the vicinity of the Persian Gulf, attracted perhaps by the civilization already existing there. The Chaldæan tradition was that the arts of civilization, writing included, had been introduced by sea, and the most recent researches and discoveries go far to show that the Chaldean historian, Berosus, who has preserved the tradition, was right. They assimilated to themselves this previous civilization, which under their influence was developed and deeply modified in the region of the country they occupied. It was also transformed and modified, *perhaps contemporaneously* during a certain period, by the Semites, in whose hands it remained at last entirely. And it was this mixed civilization which, after twenty or more centuries of evolution and wear, extended eastwards unto the borders of the Elamite country where the Bak tribes, or *Bak sings*, the future civilizers of China, could avail themselves of its advantages, about 2500 B.C.[1] Besides the inference derived from the traditions, the date is ascertained by the fact that the forms of the ancient Babylonian characters, semi-linear

---

[1] Recent discoveries (1891) in the ancient country of Illibi (Ellibi, Lilubi) in the south of Media, show that it was under the sway of Babylonian civilisation at the time of Gudea, if not before. *Cf.* G. Maspéro, *Découverte de deux Antiques monuments Chaldéens*; C. R. Acad. Inscr., t. xix. p. 426; J. de Morgan et Fr. V. Scheil, *Les deux stèles de Zohab*: Rec. de travaux, xiv. 100-106.—Gudea himself made a campaign in Elam and conquered the town of Anzan. *Cf.* the inscription of his statue B, col. vi.; *Record of the past*, 1890, vol. ii. p. 82 (tr. A. Amiaud).

and cuneiform, from which the early Chinese symbols have been derived, were those in use between the ages of Gudea and Khammurabi.[1]

132. The approximate date when the future civilisers of China[2] began their migration eastwards is known only from a supputation of traditions made by native scholars. Hu Nak Khunte (in Chinese Yu Nai Hwang-ti), was their first leader towards 2332 B.C. He raised in arms and fought with success against the successors of Sargon (in Chinese Shen nung), because his people objected to pay heavy taxes newly imposed upon them.[3] Fifty years later, *i.e.* about 2282 B.C., he had reached with his followers the south-east of the present Shensi province, and could offer a sacrifice on the banks of the Loh river.[4]

133. It would be rather bold to assert that, when fleeing east the Elamo-Babylonian yoke, and finally reaching the Flowery Land whose fame had attracted them, the leaders of the Bak Sings had actually carried away with them some written documents. It is not improbable, but we cannot prove it. In any case, it is most certain that some of the notions they had borrowed were still very fresh when they committed them to writing, and thus handed them down to posterity. Others on the contrary were rather confused in their memory. The difference in some cases may have resulted from the indirect way they had learned them.

134. The simple fact which underlies the whole history of their after-evolution and progress is that they carried away with them a semi-practical knowledge of the whole system of Elamo-Babylonian civilization in the very stage of development that had been reached a little after the middle of the

---

[1] Mr. C. J. Ball, in his independent comparisons, has come to the same conclusion.

[2] They were most probably a blue-eyed, ruddy faced, and not black-haired race. *Cf.* the demonstration in T. de L., *The Black heads of Babylonia and Ancient China*, 1892, §§ 14-20.

[3] *Cf.* T. de L., *Onomastic similarity*, § 5 ; *From Ancient Chaldea to early China*, 1891, § 46.

[4] *Cf.* Hwang P'u-mi, *Ti Wang she ki ; Nien lih*. This great scholar who lived in the third century established the chronology of olden times chiefly from traditional data, and did not subordinate his dates to the recurrence of astronomical events falsely established and calculated, as did Szema Tsien and others.

third Millenium B.C., neither before, afterwards, or elsewhere. In a special work on the *Origin of the Early Chinese civilization from Babylonia, Elam, and later western sources*,[1] besides a certain number of monographs, since the proceeding pages have been printed, I have attempted to discriminate from the subsequent acquisitions made through various channels the items of civilization in (1) sciences and arts, (2) writing and literature, (3) institutions and religion, (4) historical legends and traditions, which received by the Bak Sings previously to their migration, have belonged to them since their settlement under Yu nai Hwang-ti in the N.W. of the Flowery Land. The list includes more than one hundred different entries.

III.

135. One of the most striking evidences of this early borrowing is that which has been preserved in the astronomical statements of the first chapter of the *Shu-King* and the legendary statement of the second chapter of the *Yh-King*, as shown by the derivation of the symbols for the cardinal points from those of Chaldæa and Elam.[2] Palæographical comparisons of the ancient Babylonian characters of about 2500 B.C. with the primitive Chinese symbols, show that the signs of the diagonal Orientation of Chaldea and Elam have been the antecedents of those of the perpendicular Orientation of China as follows:

Tung, the East, and the *Left*, has been derived from *Alu*, the South-east and the *Left*.

Si, the West, and the *Right*, has been derived from *sidi*, the North-West and the *Right*.

Peh, the North and the *Back*, has been derived from *Mar(tu)*, the *Abode* (of Sunset), the South-West and *front* for the Akkado-Sumerians, and the West or *behind* for the Assyrians.

---

[1] In course of publication in *The Babylonian and Oriental Record* since February, 1889.

[2] Cited *supra*, p. 96.—*Cf*. T. de L., *From Elam to China, the shifted cardinal points*: Babylonian and Oriental Record, Jan., 1888; *From Ancient Chaldea and Elam to Early China*, par. 20-32: *Shifting of the cardinal points*: ibid. February, 1891.

Nan, the South and the *Front*, was derived from *Kurra*, the North-East and the *Back* of the Akkado-Sumerians, the East and *Front* of the Assyrians.

136. Now when the Bak Sings emigrated from their former settlements in the borders of Elam to go north-eastwards, they left behind them the *Mar* or abode, whose symbol became equivalent to their back. The fluctuations of their route caused them to forget that it ever had anything to do with the setting sun. And afterwards, bending their route southwards to reach the much coveted Flowery Land, their back became the north, and it has remained so for them. For the same reason the sign primitively *Kurra*, which they called *Nam* or *Lam*, modern *Nan*, became that of the South and their front.

This change of front implied necessarily a corresponding inversion in the two other symbols $Alu = Tung =$ Left, and $Sidi = Si =$ Right, which ought to have become the Right and the Left, inversely of what they are. But with their ancient respective meanings of Left and Right, they could be but in constant use; routine was stronger than any reasoning, and thus preserved their old and popular acceptations. The result was a curious confusion at the beginning, illustrated in the two cases we refer to, which has baffled hitherto all native and European commentators.

137. In the first chapter of the *Shu-King* it is reported that *Ti Yas* taught his followers and subjects which stars they ought to observe in order to determinate the seasons. In the North for winter it was *Mao* (Pleiades); in the South for summer, *Ho* (Scorpio); in *Tung* the East for spring, *Niao* (Hydra); and in *Si* the West for Autumn, *Hiu* (Aquarius). Now this is just the reverse of what the things are in nature, and it gives to Spring the constellations corresponding to Autumn, and *vice versa*, &c. The mistake has given to the Chinese cosmography of later years its ludicrous and unexplained appearance. Native and European astronomers agree to say that at the time of Yao, the positions of the four stars could not be all that which the text ascribes to them. The Northern observation could be made at a certain hour, but

those of the East and West were impossible. As stated by Siu-fah, the learned author of the *T'ien yuen Lih li tsiuen shu* (published in 1682), the stars such as *Hydra* ought to have changed from left to right.[1] With the data supplied to us by the antecedents of the Chinese symbols for the points of space, this gives us a clue to the right explanation which the statement of the *Yh-King* also confirms.

138. The original and concise document made use of by the Chinese leader, placing the star *Hiu* in relation with the symbol of space *Si*, and the star *Niao* with *Tung* was certainly right and logical with the things that ought to be; for, the symbols *peh* and *nan* having been inverted in meaning, *Si* and *Tung* ought also to have been inverted; the popular routine ought not to have been followed, and the inversion of meaning which consistency required agreed with the natural position of the stars. But somebody blundered with the document. The statement in the *Yh-King*, which we shall examine presently, offering the same particularity, would suggest that the error was not Yao's fault. It was more probably a mistake of the author of the chapter of the *Shu King*, who, as stated in the text, compiled it afterwards on notes from antiquity, and, unaware of the peculiarity, combined or corrected wrongly the information.

139. In the second chapter of the *Yh-King*, about the Earth, it is stated that in the *Si-nan* they got the falling down, and in the *Tung-peh* they grieved for it. With the usual acceptation of south-west and north-east for the two expressions, the statement is unintelligible. But if we look upon it as a fragment of the earliest lore written by one of the first leaders, when *Si* and *Tung* had exchanged their former acceptation like *Peh* and *Nan*, the matter becomes clear. The statement means that in the south-east they got the falling down and in the north-west they grieved for it. And it agrees with the following circumstance in the remains

---

[1] *Cf.* G. Schlegel, *Uranographie Chinoise*, 1875, pp. 4-9.—J. Chalmers, *On the Astronomy of the Ancient Chinese*, 1875.—The two European scholars agree with the Chinese.

of the Deluge legend preserved in China, verses 5, 6 and 7:[1]
"The pillars of Heaven were broken and the four cardinal points of the earth sundered;
"This caused the Heavens to fall on the *North-West*, and consequently the sun, moon and stars moved to that point;
"The Earth also became defective on the *South-East*, and that is the reason why the rivers flow in that direction."[2]

The statements of the *Shu King* and of the *Yh-King* thus explain and confirm one another, and may be looked upon as original relics of the written teachings imparted to their subjects in China by the early leaders arrived from the west.

IV.

140. We find still in the present time, although in a fragmentary and corrupted condition, some remains of traditions and legends originally from the west, which must have been taught also by the early leaders, and committed to writing for preservation. Such documents were made use of by the authors of the *Yhs*, as proved by the fragments of the *Kwei tsang* and some of the allusions referred to in the *Chöu Yh*, such as the female-animal in cosmogony, the sundering of the cardinal points, the defeat in Tsung Kiu, &c. We have investigated a few of them, such as those concerning the Deluge tradition, the Fishmen bearers of writing, the Tree of Life, Stories about Sargon (in Chinese Shennung), and Hu Nak Khunte, the animal mother in cosmogony, a list of Akkadian and Kassite Kings, with the probability of finding some more.[3] The fate of these precious relics of Western

---

[1] *Cf.* T. de L., *The Deluge Tradition and its Remains in Ancient China*, 1890, § 26 (B. and O. R., iv. 80).
[2] Allusion to the direction of the two great Mesopotamian rivers which runs from N.W. to S.E.
[3] *Cf.* T. de L., *Early History of Chinese civilisation*, 1880; *Chinese and Akkadian affinities:* The Acad. 20 Jan. 1883; *The Affinity of the ten stems of the Chinese cycle with the Akkadian numerals:* ibid. 1 Sept. 1883; *The zodiac and cycles of Babylonia and their Chinese derivatives:* ibid. 11 Oct. 1890; *The Chinese mythical Kings and the Babylonian canon:* ibid. 6 Oct. 1883; *Traditions of Babylonia in Early Chinese documents:* ibid. 17 Nov. 1883; *Babylonian and old Chinese measures:* ibid. 10 Oct. 1885; *Ancient Chinese Weights and Measures*, pp. xli-xlvi, Introd. of *Catalogue of Chinese Coins*, 1892; *Babylonia and China:* The Acad. 7 Aug. 1886; *Western origin of the early Chinese civili-*

antiquity in Ancient China was very sad. The Chinese mind in its matter-of-fact character and limited aspirations is ill-disposed to take interest in such matters. They remained, as chance permitted, more or less badly preserved in the Royal Archives, and perhaps represented only by a few copies until some circumstances roused the native mind from its slumber and attracted upon them the attention of a few.

141. About the close of the sixth century B.C., Lao Tan, who was keeper of the Royal Archives of Chöu, at Loh, found there a collection of literary remains attributed to Hwang-ti (Hu Nak Kunte) the first leader of the Bak Sings in China, and extracted from it the animal mother cosmogony to which he gave vent in the chapter sixth of his *Tao teh King*. We have seen some traces of it in the *Yh-King* (cf. Introduction). Attention began henceforth to be drawn on these long forgotten documents.

142. In the East of China around the South of the Shantung peninsula an important movement had begun since the previous century. Foreign traders of the Erythæan Sea, incited by the introduction among them of the Phœnician Navy by Sennacherib in 697–695, had pursued their maritime enterprises much further than before, and about 675 B.C. they had reached the Southern shores of Shantung, where they founded, on the gulf of Kiao-tchou, Lang-ga and Tsi-moh. It was in the latter place that the first coin of China[1] was issued by them about 670. These foreigners, Sabœans, Syrians and Hindus introduced new notions, such as astrology and superstitions, and by their sailors' yarns

---

zation : Babylonian and Oriental Record, June 1887 ; *The Chinese intruders*, par. 197-208 of *The Languages of China before the Chinese*, 1887 ; *The wheat indigenous to Mesopotamia carried to early China*, 1883 ; *The Tree of Life and the calendar plant of Babylonia and China*, 1888 ; *The calendar plant of China, the cosmic tree and the date palm of Babylonia*, 1890 ; *The legendary fishmen of early Babylonia in ancient Chinese fables*, 1888 ; *The Onomastic similarity of Nai Hwangti of China and Nakhunte of Susiana*, 1890 ; *The Deluge tradition and its remains in Ancient China*, 1890 ; *From Ancient Chaldæa and Elam to Early China, an historical loan of culture*, 1891 ; *The Black-heads of Babylonia and Ancient China*, 1892, etc. Cf. also W. St. Chad. Boscawen, *Shennung and Sargon* : B. and O. R. August 1888.

[1] Cf. T. de L., *Catalogue of Chinese coins from the 7th cent. B.C. to A.D. 621*, p. xi., lx., and 214.

awakened a curiosity for the wonderful. The social and political condition of the country was favourable to a movement of this sort. The Chinese princes were anxious of novelty to show their independence from the once respected and now disregarded suzerainty of the Kings of Chöu. It was really an age of wonderism.

143. The thinkers and philosophers who took the lead of the movement sought eagerly for the old documents of Hwang-ti, and combined the old with the new information in their speculations. But the national mind did not accept easily all these innovations, and found its most complete expression in the teachings of Confucius and his school, who objected to anything that was not tangible and well ascertained. The Taoists of Honan and the Wonderists of Shantung thus opposed could but gradually fuse together, and the result was, what has been well called, the Taoszeism, which like the Confucianism, is still at present existing in China. Now the Confucianism from its closer touch with the national character has generally, with few temporary exceptions, kept the upper hand with the Government and the literati, and thus thrown in disfavour the elucubrations and even the more sober works of the other school, including the old relics of primitive times. These relics, disdained therefore by the Confucianists, have not received all the attention they deserved and which a wholesome competition between the two schools would have secured to them. They remained at the sole disposal of the Taoseists and of non-Confucianists; the former especially to whom we are indebted for their preservation, have enlarged upon them, and in transmitting them have added wonderful accounts and details foreign to the originals, which Sinologists and modern critics have now the unwieldy task to discriminate.

V.

144. The influence of the remarkable evolution of the Chinese writing on the fate of the original *Yh-King* has been explained to a certain extent in the third chapter of the

present volume. A few additional remarks only are necessary to complete the demonstration.

The writing learned by the Bak families in the West[1] was in a hieratic stage of semi-phonetism and semi-ideographism; their faded hieroglyphism lost in some cases was in others concealed only by the stiffness of the lapidary and conventional cuneiform style; when written with the rounded strokes allowed by a soft and vegetable material as that used by the Baks, many of the symbols still preserved a distinctive appearance of their *alleged* or *original* object. The cuneiform style was not unknown to the early Chinese by tradition and also probably by some material evidence, as shown by the various traditions and monumental data (isolate survivals), which we have been able to adduce together on the subject.[2]

145. The old age of this writing, not so much however as its former (though not primitive) heterogeneous ambients Kushite, Akkadian and Semitic, had caused its characters to be used much beyond the scope of their original purposes. And many symbols, even among those whose semi-pictorial appearance was not extinct, had acquired some acceptations which could be learned but by experience and long practice. These conditions made imperative the use of explanatory lists, ideographical and phonetical, giving the various acceptations of the written characters in Assyro-Babylonia, whence the so-called syllabaries in Cuneiform characters. Now the leaders of the Bak families were under that respect, in still more stringent conditions, when they introduced this same writing in the Flowery Land. They could not help making similar lists for the teaching of their followers and new people, and some of these lists have found their way into the *Yh-King*, a contention we have held since the beginnings of

---

[1] Apparently for the first time under the reign of the Akkadian King Dungi. *Cf.* T. de L., *The Old Babylonian Characters and their Chinese derivates*, 1888, § 30. Also *The Babylonian origin of the Chinese characters*, J.R.A.S. 1888, xx. 312-315; *Chips of Babylonian and Chinese palæography*, 1888.—And the approbative paper of Prof. A. H. Sayce, *The Old Babylonian characters and their Chinese derivates*, Nature, 7 June, 1888, and B. and O. R., August, 1888.

[2] *The old Babylonian characters*, § 29; *From Ancient Chaldæa and Elam to early China*, § 19.

our decipherment of this oldest book of the Chinese. Their lists made soon after their arrival in China, could not, especially in the case of certain symbols, particularly difficult and extensively used, but contain many of the acceptations that were current for the same symbols in the West.

146. In the pp. 77–80 of the present volume, we have given a translation of the xxxth chapter of the *Yh-King* which is one of these lists concerning the symbol *Li* 离, and p. 98 a provincial list of the acceptations hitherto ascertained for the antecedent of the same symbol in the Babylonian world, *Lu*, 囼 The provisory list was short and covered but one part of the meanings indicated in the *Yh*. We had, however, been able to show as one of the original meanings, that of "Cow," which a distinguished Assyriologist had been able subsequently to find also in the Cuneiform documents at his disposal. Since then Assyriology has made some progresses, more materials have come to hand, and extensive lists have been published. It is therefore a great satisfaction for me, as it cannot fail to strengthen the confidence of our readers in our mode of dealing with the *Yh*, to give now the following comparative lists of the acceptations of this symbol in the cuneiform texts, and of those which attributed to its derivate by the leaders of the Bak families in China have found their way into the *Yh*.

147. The sources referred to are for the Babylonian side the most useful *Classified List of all simple and compound Cuneiform Ideographs*, published in 1889 by Dr. Rudolph E. Brünnow. It contains no less that 27 entries for the character in question alone with as many different Assyro-Babylonian equivalents,[1] some of which are duplicate meanings. I subjoin the numero of the entry to each quotation. For the Chinese I have taken the 22 meanings of the chapter 30th of the *Yh* above, reducible to 16 because of six duplicates, and I subjoin also the serial number for reference in every case.

---

[1] As the translations are not given in this work, I have referred for them to the vocabularies of F. Delitzsch, J. Halevy, P. Haupt, F. Lenormant, J. Oppert, T. G. Pinches, A. H. Sayce, and special information from Prof. Fritz Hömmel.

THE YH-KING AND ITS AUTHORS.

BABYLONIAN.	CHINESE.
10678, *bûlu*, cattle; 10697, *sênu*, sheep; p. 98 . . . . cow.	1. A domestic cow.
10675, *alaku* . . . . . to walk.	2. To shoe.
10676, *ba'u* . . . . . . to seek.	3. Confused.
10688, *mitu* . . . . . to die.	4. Burn away; 7. Brightness fading; 12. Burning like; 13. Dying.
10699, *tamâḫu*, to hold; 10687, *lamû*, to surround; 10700, *yullulu*, to protect.	5. Attentive; 17. Lucky omen.
?	6. Bird.
10690, *nigû* . . . . . music.	8. Special music.
10685, *kiṣṣu* . . . . multitude.	9. Perpetual chatter.
10680, *ḫâtu*, trespass; 10679, *êtêku*, to go forward.	10. Oppose, rushing against.
10677, *ba'âru* . . . . to hunt.	11. To meet.
10694, *sabâtu*; 10695, *sibtu*; 10683, *kamû* . . . . . to seize.	14. Throwing of; 16. to split wood; 19. to cut off.
10698, *tabaku* . . . . Outpouring.	15. Falling drops.
10694, *aḫazu* . . to possess, to take	18. To have something.
10684, *kirdibbu?*; 10685, *kirru*, animal; 10681, *immeru* . . beast.	20. Ravenous beast.
10692, *kababu* . . . . . a cover.	21. Bamboo basket.
10696, *subburu* . . . to oppress.	22. Abominable (Bogie).

148. So that, with the exception of "Bird" (which may be recovered in future decipherments) all the meanings ascribed to the symbol in the *Yh-King* have been found in the documents belonging to the fountain head of the civilisation imported into China by the Bak families.

Considering the extraordinary difficulties under which these lists of meanings can be studied, scholars will appreciate how remarkable and how conclusive is the proof which we have just quoted, and which has come as an accessory after the fact.

VI.

149. When Yu Nai Hwang-ti and his followers introduced in China the system of writing they had learned in the West, the Pre-Chinese populations of the country were in possession of three sorts of embryo-writings: cup-marks, knotted-cords, and notched sticks, and there is no evidence whatever that they should have used any system of pictograph except, perhaps, as isolate symbols, but not as a body of written characters from which additional signs might have been borrowed by the scribes of the Bak families. This is shown by the simple fact, that besides the absence of any traditional

or monumental relics to the contrary, the objects of Chinese origin which were unknown to new comers, such as silk, cocoon, silkworm, iron, &c., had to be named with characters simple or compound of the imported writing. In course of time certain characters from the system imported by the Bak families, were attributed to these objects, either as descriptive symbols, or because of their outside appearance, pictograph like, of the objects, however foreign to their original purpose.[1]

150. As all the ideographical writings, the written characters of Ancient China increased in number in course of time, from their internal system, because of the wanted additions required by the progress of knowledge. But their increase took place in peculiar conditions which it is important for Sinologists to remember, because of the false inferences which the appearance of the writing would seem otherwise to justify, if not thoroughly investigated. Therefore it is highly necessary to remark that, should the writing introduced by the Baks have contained no traces of hieratic pictographs, it would have been a bar to any addition of new characters similarly made; such as it was, the contrary was the result, as the standard characters could not object to the introduction among them of new symbols distinctly framed on the principle of sketched pictographs for fresh purposes, or for clearer meaning in substitution of older and more conventional characters. Besides these voluntary additions the writing has increased from the three following sources: (1) variants resulting from the gradual neglect of the primary rules of spelling and composition, and the actual ignorance and carelessness of the scribes; (2) local variants of the standard forms, entered into the vocabulary with an acquired shade of meaning; (3) pictorial equivalents of difficult or little known standard characters, actually created among the less cultivated part of the Chinese dominion. These various causes of alterations and increase of the written vocabulary continued

---

[1] The Bak families knew GOLD, COPPER, SILVER and TIN (or antimony) from their western residence; they did not know BRONZE which reached them from the west in the eighteenth century, nor IRON which they learned from the Pre-Chinese, and which they called for that reason the barbarian metal. Cf. *Catalogue of Chinese Coins*, pp. viii. and xxii.

to act even after the famous ideographical renovation of the writing of 820 B.C. which we have described, p. 21, and which was certainly not calculated to put a stop to them.

We hope that the foregoing statements of facts and explanations will dissipate the illusions of those who might be inclined to believe in a self-grown and hieroglyphical origin of the Chinese writing, and therefore refuse to study our explanation of the not uncomplicated problem hitherto unsolvable of the *Yh-King*.

www.ingramcontent.com/pod-product-compliance
Lightning Source LLC
Chambersburg PA
CBHW030347170426
43202CB00010B/1273